MASTER LOVERS

a twisted puzzle of
love and fascism

DAVID WINNER

Outpost19 | San Francisco
outpost19.com

Winner, David
Master Lovers / David Winner
ISBN 9781944853884

Available in paperback and ebook editions.

OUTPOST19

SAN FRANCISCO

MASTER LOVERS

"David Winner calls his book a fictional memoir, which it is—though it's more than that. He doesn't just imagine dialogue he couldn't have overheard, he reveals himself to be a full (if surprised) participant in someone else's life that shapes his own, as he comes to better understand his beloved relative. Dorle is always boldly present, her yearning for the here and now mixed with some other, more meaningful scenario not easily available to women of her time. She was daring, and so is her biographer, who remains pretty convincingly absent until he returns to dance a final pas de deux with his subject.

"I loved those times when David popped up, to quickly offer his own concise opinion about Dorle's suitors, for example. I could also understand his wife's perspective—only briefly touched on—about the volume of material he brings into their apartment in his obsession to sort through it, to study it in terms of text and subtext, and to —it turns out—shape what might otherwise have been lost material into this amazing book.

"In this time of everyone's fascination with genealogical research, and amid the tattered prose of Twitter, it seems particularly daring to write so eloquently, comprehensively, and fearlessly about someone whose wanderlust was paired with a lust for love as an end in itself; she was (as my grandmother would have said) a woman 'ahead of her time.' What interesting person isn't?

"Certainly the props helped: shipboard romances; exotic places. In actual documents and sometimes in invented dialogue, a complicated view of society emerges that is not limited to the consideration of one singular woman's life. It's as if F. Scott Fitzgerald had stopped the action of Gatsby at the big party in order to give us deep background on every flashy attendee, until the mystery of what gives life meaning implicated everyone in Gatsby's orbit. Gatsby is a mystery—one that Nick Carraway is there to observe. I can't help thinking that without her grandnephew, David, Dorle, too, might have been lost to us.

"This book is a brilliant concoction, equal to the ingredients that might have been combined in Dorle's cocktail shaker: fact, fiction, revelation, riddles. It has a sad ending – though one that is so kind. The tenderness broke my heart."
— **Ann Beattie**, winner of the PEN/
Malamud Award and the Rea Award
for the Short Story

"Through compassion, doggedness, imagination, and an utter absence of sentimentality, David Winner gives us an unforgettable portrait of both a spirited, flawed, mysterious woman and a fascinating era that is no more. Master Lovers is a gem."
— **Clifford Thompson,** author of *What It Is: Race, Family, and One Thinking Black Man's Blues* and *Big Man and the Little Men: A Graphic Novel*

MASTER
LOVERS

FOREWORD

While clearing out my great-aunt Dorle's Midtown Manhattan apartment after her death, I discovered artifacts of her storied existence: notes
from opera stars, love letters, artifacts from the
Middle East of the 1930's, but the more I learned
about her and her world, the more complicated
things became.

The sentimental story of Dorle, her lovers,
and her classical music demi-monde seemed like
an escape from these ominous times until I happened to pull a rock out from on top of it and
found a twisted puzzle full of fascism and fraud.

Dorle, an Orthodox Jew, met an American
reporter named John Carter on the *Île-de-France*
sailing from Le Havre to New York in 1932, and
soon they embarked on a tumultuous affair nearly five years in duration. But less than ten days
before their romantic encounter up in the funnels of the ship, Carter and his wife, Sheila, had
witnessed in person the fall of the Reichstag and
listened to Hitler decry the Jews at a rally, which
Sheila referred to in her diary as a "quite a good
show." Later, Carter would announce to Dorle
that he'd met with George Viereck, a man responsible for deluging much of America with pro-
German propaganda in the years leading up to
World War II, the "top banana" among German
influencers in America, according to Rachel Maddow in her fall 2022 *Ultra* podcast.

There are extenuating circumstances. Nothing about this appears in any of the hundreds of letters that Carter wrote Dorle, which allows me to hope that she never knew. Still, Dorle, a Jewish liberal who'd contributed to the defense funds of Sacco and Vanzetti and the Scottsboro Boys, had been at only one degree of separation from Adolf Hitler.

And Dorle had other lovers, all committed to politics at different extremes, from colonial Palestine and Syria to the Spanish Civil War. Dorle had a thing for men in power. She also held to sexual mores that can still raise eyebrows.

Despite love and its distractions, Dorle (Jarmel Soria), had a brilliant career. One of the first female students at Columbia Journalism School when it granted undergraduate degrees, she eventually became press manager of what would become Columbia Artists Management. Under their aegis, she managed the New York Philharmonic, playing a key role in the careers of Arturo Toscanini, who wrote her many letters, and Leonard Bernstein, whose debut she helped coordinate. In 1942, she married Dario Soria, an Italian Jew who had emigrated from Italy in advance of the Holocaust. Together, they formed a boutique classical record label called Angel Records. While with Angel, they grew close to Maria Callas, arranging both her Metropolitan and Chicago Lyric Opera debuts and fielding agonized calls from Meneghini, her husband, after Maria had left him for Aristotle Onassis. And receiving a terse letter from Callas herself years later after Onassis had abandoned her for Jacqueline, "as for Daddy O, what is over is over, Sagittarians are like that."

Having declared in her diary at sixteen that "there is nothing like work as a shield and a comforter," Dorle kept writing the column called "Artist Life" that she'd started in the 1950s and directing the archiving of classic performances of the Metropolitan Opera until well into her nineties.

Dorle transcended expectations of culture and of gender, but what do we do with the evil hovering around her? Do we hold her responsible for her bedfellows or condone her as an actor typical of her time? If there had been a congressional anti-Americanism committee rooting out fascism and dictatorship rather than communism, what would she say in her defense should she have been called as a witness?

She and Dario did champion Black opera singers Leontyne Price and Marian Anderson in the sixties and seventies. And when Price got a terrible taste of her native Mississippi, asked to take the service elevator up to Dorle and Dario's apartment, Dorle and Dario managed to expunge that racist policy.

But there was also the matter of Dorle's celebration of the Nazi-associated musicians so important to the postwar musical landscape, and writing this book brought me face-to-face with other questionable connections: her lovers, her husband, her father, her uncle, her brother-in-law.

And if we consider guilt by association, there is me to contend with. My late parents and

I have led unremarkable lives, enjoying the proximity of Dorle's opulent existence without considering the ethically ambiguous flip side. Both the fictions she wrote as a teenager and her real-life love affairs were populated by powerful men, and in those times, like these times, powerful men live shadowy lives.

TABLE OF CONTENTS

CHAPTER ONE
DISCOVERIES

Every January and June during my childhood, my mother would drive my father and me from Charlottesville to Manhattan in the old family Datsun. We'd stay with my great-aunt Dorle and her Rome-born husband Dario in their large mid-century modern apartment on 55th Street. I'd be pampered with giant gingerbread houses and candy canes and taken to old-fashioned French and Italian restaurants with elaborate dessert trays.

By the end of my twenties when I landed in New York myself, Dario was over a decade dead but Dorle (in her nineties) was very much alive.

On Friday nights throughout much of the 1990s, my girlfriend, now wife, Angela, and I would subway from Brooklyn to have cocktails and dinner with Dorle.

We'd request anecdotes about long-gone friends from her jeweled past. In rapt breathless tones, she would take us back to winter Long Island in the twenties where young Vladimir Horowitz imagined the howling of wolves, sixties Paris, where Maria Callas lay, desolate and bed-bound, in her apartment after Onassis left her for Jacqueline.

A lifelong romantic, Dorle had supposedly published love stories of her own in her early youth. After her death in 2002 at the age of 101, I found them among her papers.

Written in the 1910s when she was in her teens, *Master Lovers of the World* was loosely based on the lives of historical figures.

In Dorle's telling, Irish nationalist Charles Steward Parnell had his heart broken three times. First by a "young girl picking plums in an orchard" with a "delicate rose-flushed face with its golden hair … framed in a sunbonnet." She drowned.

His second love was encountered at a "Fifth Avenue ballroom" with a "rainbow froth of dancers." Her hair was "piled high in auburn masses, her eyes were hazel" and "shot with golden lights" but she would not marry him "until he distinguished himself." A year after Parnell "slaved in the cause of Irish freedom, he learned via telegram of the marriage of his fickle betrothed to another man."

When he fell in love with Kitty, "the wife of his political follower, Captain O'Shea," they "fought desperately [but unsuccessfully] against the devastating passion which threatened to engulf them."

Parnell sent a letter daily and two telegrams, "one to bid her good morning and another to wish her goodnight." In 1890, ten years before Dorle's own birth, "the storm broke." Captain O'Shea sued for divorce, and the ensuing scandal detonated a "bomb in the Irish ranks."

"For good or for ill," Dorle has him writing Kitty, "I am your husband, your love, your child, your all. And I will give my life for Ireland but to you I will give my love."

Dorle's Parnell, a "beloved leader," was as sweet as he was heroic. But her other master lovers could be capricious, unkind. "With casual cruelty," Beau Brummell, the Prince of Dandies, told a woman with curvature of the spine who had just returned from Paris that she "must have been damnably warped by the way."

"Painter and Pagan," Paul Gauguin emerged at night, "paint-stained, savage, reserved, and drank green liquor and made indifferent love to his adoring models." When he returned from a journey to Martinique, he filled his studio with "wooden clubs and spears and two monkeys. And he kept as a model a mulatto woman who worshipped him like a slave!"

"Master François Villon, Prince of Bohemia … [was a] poet, thief, vagabond and master lover! … Time and again, he kissed and loved and vanished into the black depths of the underworld."

And Franz Liszt, "was God and Lucifer and Don Juan."

What happened, I began to wonder, when the adolescent mistress of master lovers began to have romantic entanglements of her own? Did she have real lovers as powerful and cruel as her fictional ones? Born to a nineteenth-century Orthodox Jewish family, Dorle should have been married young and concentrated on housekeeping, but her professional career lasted until her nineties, and she remained single until the end of her thirties.

A series of discoveries—some exciting, some confusing, some discouraging—answered many of my questions about her earlier life.

I came across *Master Lovers* after Dorle's death in the summer of 2002, when my parents sold one of the two adjacent apartments in which she had lived since the 1940s, but I would have to wait until 2010, when my father sold the second apartment, to gain access to drawers and cubbies unopened for decades.

On a sultry summer afternoon, I arrived at apartment 8C, rolled up my sleeves to begin the job of clearing things out but napped instead on a fraying sofa across from a noisy old Friedrich air-conditioner. Upon waking, I made myself a cup of dubious tea from an ancient tea bag and opened a filing cabinet, the top layer of which I'd explored before.

Previously, I'd found a framed photo of Mick Jagger yukking it up with Dorle at a party in the 1980s on which an old friend had scrawled, "Eat your heart out, Pavarotti." A typed note from Paul Bowles, right under it, invited Dorle to Tangier. When she took him up on it, she tried hashish marmalade like the good sport she always was. Below the Bowles letter was a frayed address book from the early 1970s, which included Diana Ross and Benny Goodman.

Below them, two yellowed copies of the *New York Times* had been stuffed inside. I paged through them as best I could, but none of the stories seemed relevant to Dorle, and I was scattering little bits of paper all over the old carpet. Once

I'd fully removed the newspapers, I saw that they served as a peculiar barrier. Hidden below them lay hundreds of mysterious gray envelopes, letters to Dorle sent from a Washington, DC, address from someone called John Carter.

When I tried to read one from October of 1934, about six years before Dorle met Dario, the handwriting crystalized and a reason for hiding the letters grew clear.

"Dear Dorle, by one of those last-minute flukes which makes reason reel, I am to be accompanied on my next trip to New York. I don't think I've ever been so miserable in all my life, and I know you will be terribly hurt. On Thursday morning, I shall telephone, and I may be able to find a way of seeing you."

John's misery in being accompanied suggested that Dorle (like the redoubtable Kitty from her Charles Parnell romance) had been sleeping with a married man.

"What I or life can do with our love," John concluded, "is still beyond my power to guess, but it is still there, stronger than ever."

The deeper I dug into the filing cabinet, the more letters from John I discovered, cascades of tormented love, ripe with melodramatic words like those Dorle had placed inside the mouths of her master lovers.

I Googled John Carter over and over, but it was too common a name to yield anything relevant until finding his full name, "John Franklin Carter," scrawled in Dorle's hand on a manila envelope containing yet more letters, provided some basic details. A journalist and bureaucrat, he'd worked with FDR on the New Deal then spied for him during the war.

In the days and weeks that followed, I searched the apartment for more secrets. Dorle had returned from a trip to India in the early 1960s with an enormous wooden cabinet on which episodes from the life of Krishna had been elaborately carved. A decorative object without obvious practical purpose, it had always stayed closed.

After pulling open its creaky door, I found it empty, save more yellowing newspapers. But deep inside the newspapers, I found an old cigar box. Inside, there was another set of love letters from the 1930s from a man named Bill Barker. That name, like Carter's, was too common to easily trace, but the initials A.T. Barker on one of the envelopes revealed him to be Alfred Tennyson Barker, a British soldier and policeman who had fought in Gallipoli, Ireland, and the Middle East.

In the weeks that followed, as I forayed from Brooklyn to Manhattan to go through Dorle's possessions, I discovered three more sets of love letters from the 1930s. All told, there were three Brits (J.B.S. Haldane, Albert Coates, Bill Barker), one Syrian (Georges Asfar), and one American (John Carter). Haldane, Coates, and Carter were married. Barker and Asfar were not.

Later, as I worked my way through the difficult handwriting and florid prose of Dorle's lovers, I began to wonder about these affairs. Where did they begin? Where did they end? At least five times in the 1930s, she must have crushed hearts and/or experienced the crushing of her own.

Though full of striking details, the letters left basic questions unanswered. I began to wish that Dorle had written an autobiographical second volume of her *Master Lovers* book detailing what happened between her and these men. From the letters, I learned the sorry story of John Carter's drunken syphilitic brother and the woman he was slated to marry, but not what exactly transpired between John, his wife Sheila and Dorle. I discovered (from both the letters and an article in the *New York Times*) a lawsuit threatening Georges Asfar's antiquities business, but not where, how, and when Georges and Dorle met.

Some useful clues emerged in the plastic bins where I eventually threw the papers that I found in her apartment: letters to her mother from the 1930s in which she talked about her lovers, her poignant teenage diary, written as American troops were gathering in New York to go off to the First World War, and, of course, in her *Master Lovers* stories themselves.

Dorle described the court of Louis XIV as filled with love "in a thousand and one intoxicating forms," like the stories of Scheherazade that transfixed her as a child.

I don't have near that many tales to relate, only five: Bill, the Gallipoli survivor; John, the New Dealer; Georges, the Ottoman antiquities salesman; Haldane, a founder of population genetics who cured tetanus and fought Franco. The most enigmatic ones (from the conductor Albert Coates) were discovered in Dorle's dresser drawers but addressed to a mysterious entity known as "Joanny" whose trail I tried to follow.

What I could piece together about these love affairs took me on a journey through Dorle's life from her love-filled, lovelorn twenties and thirties through her marriage to Dario, to the nineties when I really got to know her.

The quotations from the letters are only lighted edited for clarity, but the gaps in the stories are filled in by pure speculation.

We will begin with Dorle's brief encounter with the British soldier and police officer Bill Barker. Easily the most cinematic of her lovers, he'd been governing a large swath of British Mandate Palestine during the Arab Revolts of the 1930s.

His letters to Dorle were sweet, sincere. He saw himself as keeping the peace rather than imposing colonial power. "I am in a land," he wrote, "where innocent people, Jews, and Arabs, women and children are blown to pieces by bombs, lives of people whose only crime is race destroyed by assassins who only know them to be of the race they hate."

Bill's bravery and fortitude recalls Dorle's beloved Irish nationalist, Charles Parnell. Soon after Parnell's death, writes Dorle, "it was whispered that somewhere in the green hills he waited, his flaming eyes, which had fired the cause of freedom, smoldering, his silvery voice which had drawn his followers like the Pied Piper of old, stilled, until the day of Ireland's greatest need." Bill, on the other hand, had been a member of that brutal colonialist British police force in Ireland, the Black and Tans.

But both men may have been crushed by love. "Parnell might be alive today," writes Dorle, "if it were not for the three love tragedies which hastened his death." And Bill, agonized by the loss of Dorle in the 1930s, lived for three more decades without marrying.

Dorle and Bill chanced across each other on the Austrian Lloyd Triestino ship en route from Trieste to Haifa in the spring of 1934. Dorle had dropped by her old haunts—Paris, Salzburg, Rome—on her way to meet Georges Asfar in the Middle East, a place she'd dreamt of since reading *The Arabian Nights* as a child gave birth to a lifetime of Orientalism.

CHAPTER TWO
THE FAIRLY GOOD POLICEMAN

The Lloyd Triestino Line

The first port of call is Venice, a distance of some eighty miles, which should take them only a few hours. Dorle's first order of business is to unpack what she plans to wear on the voyage into the dresser drawers of her cabin. Then she hangs up the dress she plans for dinner—what she has on now will do for lunch—and sets up her make-up kit in the tiny bathroom.

Once that's done, she takes a quick tour of the ship, concluding with the funnels, which—another year, another boat—she'd visited with John Franklin Carter.

After the boat docks in Venice, acquires more passengers, and sets sail again, she heads to the dining room for luncheon.

The expression on her face as she sits down at a table for four will be described by Bill Barker years later as a mixture of "immense hurt with terrific fright."

"Perhaps it's neither," he will go on, "but fleetingly you seemed like a wounded animal at bay."

Her turbulent affair with John Carter may be on her mind. She may be returning to Georges Asfar to try to drain Carter from her system.

But Dorle is innately social. While introducing herself to the three men who will be her companions at meals for the next several days, she rises to the occasion. Bill will describe the three of them singing Dorle's praises.

"I speak with authority," Bill writes. "You have passed a very critical board (a) a captain who has sailed before the masts, (b), a mining engineer who knows the mining camps of the world, (c), a fairly good policeman who has served four years of war; been a Black and Tan, four years a gendarme in Palestine."

They are encountering each other for the first time while the boat departs Venice en route to the Free State of Fiume (now in Croatia) on the other side of the Adriatic.

An attractive, exotic American Jewish woman looking quite a bit younger than her mid-thirties, Dorle is extremely skilled (in the opinion of a high school boyfriend) in the areas of "flirtation" and "foolish chatter." And has, according to her friend, the young George Cukor, "a genius for friendship."

Dressed in a silver frock with her curly hair bobbed in a 1920s manner, she draws each of her companions out in turn. Those not being interviewed listen and sip their wine. A great deal of Chianti is consumed.

As the ship journeys across the Adriatic, the captain — loosened by wine and a woman—fills their first meal on board with the tale of a ship nearly running aground near the Arctic and another narrowly evading pirates in the South China Sea.

Dorle and her new friends gently rock in

choppy waters, fresh bottles of Chianti magically replacing finished ones.

Her lunch companions announce their intentions to siesta, but Dorle, avid Orientalist on her way to the Orient, is too wound up to sleep.

After taking a second tour of the ship, she settles herself on a deck chair and gets out *I, Claudius*, an ancient Roman potboiler that I found on her bookshelf after her death.

Which makes perfect fodder for conversation when the also restless Bill Barker, a little woozy from the wine and the jaw pain that has been worsening over the last few days, walks by her chair just as she is getting to a juicy bit about Caligula.

Too modest to talk about orgies when asked to describe what she's reading, she tells the story of the emperor making his horse into a senator instead. Bill looks toward the Italian coast, pauses, then giggles to himself. Only in southern climes would one find such tomfoolery.

Just as the conversation sputters to a close, and Bill prepares to dart back to his cabin to avoid the embarrassment of running out of conversation with the exotic American girl who had been criss-crossing his mind since lunch, Dorle asks how he ended up as a "fairly good policeman."

Bill pauses, clears his throat, and explains how he'd enlisted in the Great War and found himself fighting the Turks at Gallipoli.

Suddenly shy again, Bill turns away from

Dorle towards the waves crashing into the sides of the boat, then looks back at her again in search of boredom or disdain. Is this proper conversation to be having with a woman? Should he really have answered her question about Palestine by going all the way back to the war? But Dorle's eyes are wide with excitement, as she's never expected to meet someone who survived Gallipoli, a man who would fit so perfectly in the Brave Heroes book she began but never completed after she'd finished her *Master Lovers*.

Bill flinches, gazes back at her transfixed face, and meekly excuses himself after explaining that he has many more tales to tell.

At dinner, as the ship passes by the coast of Abruzzo, Dorle shines her spotlight on the mining engineer. From Bill's letters, we learn his name is Tallent. He could have been John Tallent from San Francisco, who mined in Bolivia but knew, according to Bill, the "mining camps of the world."

Tallent's tales continue after the meal is consumed, and our merry quartet is drinking highballs at the bar.

As the hour grows later, bedtime looming, Dorle catches the yearning on Bill's face. Just before his eyes turn timidly towards the ground, she graces him with a smile. She knows that he wants more than the wider fellowship of the four of them and will not necessarily refuse him.

Bill rises early the next morning in his usual manner, consumes several cups of black coffee at the bar, with one teaspoon of sugar each and a crumpet without butter, and takes off to wander the ship again. Once, twice, three times, he strolls the decks, until finally, after nearly an hour, he runs into Dorle putting out a cigarette just below the funnels. Relief floods his achy body and brings him face to face with his desires. He'd been searching for her all along.

Warmly but awkwardly, he approaches her, taking her small hands inside his sweaty paws and trying to come up with a question or comment fit for her sophisticated New York Jewish life.

But after a moment of painful silence, Dorle asks him to pick up just where they'd left off, a mental bookmark having been inserted into his oral autobiography.

Upon his return to England after the war, he'd found work as a mechanic as he'd learned something of vehicles while in France. But feeling disaffected (and probably haunted by Great War nightmares), he re-enlisted after only a year or so of civilian life. Those bloody Irish were causing trouble again, and one had to do one's part.

As Bill strolls the decks with Dorle, he peers around him, hoping they don't run into the mining engineer or the captain, as the special connection he's developing with Dorle may fall by the wayside. An hour or so later, they part company with a wave and a quiet kiss upon each other's cheeks.

By early afternoon, as the ship bears upon Brindisi, Bill becomes the man of the hour in lunchtime conversation, his past heroics from Gallipoli to Ireland, his present position policing colonial Palestine.

As Britain is suppressing Arab opposition to the settling of Jews, Bill has had the occasion to meet a fair number of them. They are generally swarthier, more Oriental than Dorle, but he can recognize the Semitic qualities of her face—the nose, the cheekbones.

Later that evening, as the boat approaches the heel of Italy on its way to Greece, Bill fortifies himself with a drink of scotch neat and climbs the staircase towards the hallway in which Dorle's cabin is located, the number of which she had mentioned in passing during their private conversation earlier that day.

The offering of that information, plus the gratitude that she must feel for protecting the Jews may make her receptive. Besides, an unmarried Jewess traveling alone and befriending strange men may not hew to the normal standards.

Nevertheless, it takes several minutes of fretting and pacing outside her cabin to garner the courage to knock. And several minutes more for his jaw ache to subside enough to give him a chance of sounding articulate.

His fear of disturbing her sleep evaporates as she alertly tells him to "enter," without asking who he is.

Sitting in her nightgown at the cabin's tiny desk, she reads a dog-eared letter on yellow stationery from John Franklin Carter that she has taken on her journey.

Feeling the alcohol coursing through him and trying to channel the bravery he's shown on the battlefield, Bill rushes towards her.

"Darling Dorle," he stutters, "I couldn't stand another moment without you."

His jumbled sincerity charms her utterly. She had told John Carter she might be seeing other men, and why wait until Georges Asfar in Damascus when a handsome policeman is declaring his love in her cabin?

That evening and for the last three nights of the passage, as the boat sails from Greece towards Palestine, two different states of affairs exist among our merry quartet.

Their long Chianti-soaked lunches and dinners abound with elaborate running jokes and dramatic storytelling—Dorle, a "marvelous woman and grand," according to the mining engineer, a locus of sexual energy.

But later in the evening and once in the afternoon, Dorle and Bill find each other, drink a drop of whisky, talk a bit more, and, of course, make love.

The four become two later in the evening, but gradually, after the voyage is over and the years begin to pass—when the captain disappears, followed by the mining engineer, and Dorle ceases to respond to Bill's correspondence

—our "fairly good policeman" becomes just himself.

Their leave-taking as the ship docks in Haifa is both fraught and complex. In public, Bill receives a sturdy hug and a peck on both cheeks from Dorle and firm handshakes from the mining engineer and the captain, but earlier that morning after making love one last time, they'd clasped hold of each other like it could save them from being torn apart.

A perfectly appropriate tear creeps down Dorle's face during their public goodbye. Bill's three tears, on the other hand, are unbefitting for a war hero and a 1930s British male.

After the Passage

Bill's first letters were not mailed from Palestine but England where he is sent soon afterwards, "to have a terrific molar pulled out of my jaw."

"Bloody and unromantic, but I wish you would apply a persisting aching jaw to any moment that I appeared forgetful."

In almost every letter, Bill addresses Dorle as *"habirabi"* (beloved) and ends with *"salaam"* (hello or goodbye) written in Arabic as well as Roman lettering in order to spark her Orientalist passions.

When next he writes, he is still in England and has met up with the mining engineer.

"We talked of little else—except you—and blast him, he did most of the talking. I couldn't

18

even squeeze a word in edgeways for some time. We seemed to agree that you were a marvelous woman. We toasted you in three or four bottles of Chianti."

The two of them huddle over a dark table in a large, busy restaurant, having finished dishes of whatever passed for pasta in the Britain of the 1930s, the engineer droning on about his unrequited crush, and Bill never revealing what happened at night when the rest of the quartet were asleep.

On another Lloyd Triestino craft after his dental surgery, bound once again for Haifa, Bill writes to tell Dorle that he expects her "to appear any moment, and most marvelous woman, I shall write you of the things that are good for you."

"Hell, Dorle," he concludes, "why are you not here? The sun has just gone down over a calm sea and your presence on board would turn a heavenly setting into heaven. There are very few passengers on board, and everything is very quiet. No one drinks. No one speaks. It seems unreal and ghostly."

In a shakier pen, he drunkenly describes what happens after he consumes several sherries and goes to dine.

"At dinner, I sat alone. There was a bunch of roses and two candles opposite just in front of an empty chair. The roses represented you. They were reddish in bud, cream in flower. That's you, Dorle, I hate you. Hate you. Hate you. Why the hell are you not on board instead of putting pep in pep in Noo York? I don't know. Seriously, if you were on board tonight I would promote you. You should be above all sheep and above all fairly good goats. In fact, I would create a new category — you would be placed above all very good looking and marvelous women, well above Miss Simpson, because you, after all, are a good looking and marvelous woman."

Dorle was the model American girl, Wallis Simpson, her crass antithesis.

"P.S.," Bill plaintively concludes, "Write to me to say you don't really dislike me and minus an aching tooth, there is a chance you might really like me."

The Gare Du Nord

My father, to whom Dorle once told the story of Bill Barker, believed that the two of them had only met at sea, which was my assumption as I read his letters. But in one letter dated December 26 (no year), he makes a peculiar comment about changing trains in Paris. "I booked a sleeper from Calais to Genoa, so I had to change in Paris. I kept my blind drawn as we passed or stopped at the main station of Hell."

How can the Gare du Nord terrify a man who survived Gallipoli?

Because he had said goodbye to Dorle there for the second and final time.

We can be sure of three things about their final encounter in Paris.

It made a nightmare scape out of a train station.

They had some exchange of cash. "Once upon a time in Paris, you held two American dollars in your hand and gave them to me. It was to adjust some small payment I had made for you. It was the 12th of November of 1936, years and years and years ago."

And like most visitors to Paris, they went for a walk and dined at a restaurant. "And in my aimless wandering of Paris," he wrote when he returned in 1939, "I traced part of the walk we took, but I couldn't remember it at all nor the name of the restaurant at which we dined. I have often been tempted to ask the name of the place, but I think it would spoil it all to even peep into it without you."

Three years earlier, Bill heads from London to Paris, having recuperated from the first in a series of stomach surgeries.

He takes an early morning train to Dover, and a midday ferry to Calais.

On the ferry, he prefers the crisp deck air to the steamy and claustrophobic inside.

The ham sandwich with chips he'd consumed on the train sit heavy in his gut, and he wonders how it will handle the rich French food that he will be expected to share with Dorle and worries about making love when his stomach isn't right.

A half an hour or so into the journey, it seems to be settling down, but the rain and cold have penetrated too deeply into his bones, so, shaking and shivering, he makes his way inside.

The wooden benches on the sides of the cabin are occupied, and he has to squeeze into the middle in between a grizzled elderly man, shuffling uncomfortably and sipping from a silver flask, and a teenage French girl sucking on candy and glancing warily around her, nervous about the journey home by herself.

Though living through the Spanish flu has made a germophobe of Bill, he asks the old man for a sip, takes a long pull of backwater-flavored whisky, leans his shoulders back and closes his eyes.

And sees Dorle in his mind when he first set eyes on her, boarding the Lloyd Triestino ship in her silver frock.

Bill wakes up with a jolt, unsure where he is. The grizzled man is no longer by his side, and the sleeping teenage girl leans against his shoulder.

An announcement over the PA system lets everyone know that Calais is fast approaching. The passengers should gather their belongings and begin to queue.

It is now twilight, the sky outside perfectly clear, the gloom having been left behind in England.

The walk from the port to the train station is longer than he had expected, but the fresh air and brisk exercise should do him good.

On the train, Bill stares out at the dark French countryside destined to be a battleground again in a few short years. The other passengers near him sleep, but he stays rigidly awake, excited, frightened.

He has come up with what should be a workable plan. Dorle will be granted a final year with Toscanini, then she will move to Palestine and experience the desert firsthand—the camels, the cyclamen, the magical sound of the call to prayer. She will certainly fall in love with the place. In no more than a year, he's likely to be promoted to head the northern province and will then be provided spacious and pleasant enough housing to meet her standards, and they will be able to afford at least two Arab servants.

But what if she asks him to move to New York? He hopes that she does not.

"Forget skyscrapers, ice water, drinks, gold teeth, stockmakers, Noo York, half chewed cigars and statues of liberty. Think of camel bells, cyclamen and the last lions," he has written her.

The plan is for them to meet at an inexpensive pension near the Gare du Nord, clean and comfortable enough for sleeping and making love.

By the time the train arrives in Paris, it is one in the morning. As Bill speaks no French nor knows Paris, he hails a taxi and hands the driver a piece of paper with the address of the hotel. The driver snickers while dropping him off two short blocks away.

Bill has suggested they book two rooms for decency's sake and meet for breakfast in the morning room of the hotel at nine the next day.

"*Bonsoir,*" Bill tells the elderly lady who opens the hotel door after he's rung the bell.

"*Je suis Bill Barker,*" he goes on, employing another expression given to him by Dorle in her last letter.

She nods, shows him inside, and takes him up the stairs without grabbing a room key. Bill can hardly remedy that oversight without the language.

Up a creaky staircase, down a murky hallway, the old lady abandons him in front of room 7.

"*Madame,*" he says, rather too loudly for that hour of night.

The old lady turns around and faces him, a question mark on her face.

But "*Je suis Bill Barker*" is all he can think to say.

The old lady gestures towards the door, a cloud of annoyance at this inept Englishman settling on her face.

Suddenly the door of room 7, reserved for Bill Barker, opens and Dorle slips out. She has heard the commotion, understands the problem, and ushers Bill into the room. Having decided it was ridiculous to take separate rooms and only meet the next morning when they had only three days together, she has taken his room for them both.

The next day they stroll arm in arm from

Montmartre to Notre Dame, from the Rive Gauche to Montparnasse.

Despite Dorle's *Master Lovers* and infatuation with Swinburne, Bill is the real romantic here. Dorle is the "one true woman," like in the Sherlock Holmes story he loved in school.

Which comes home to Dorle during their leave-taking at the Gare du Nord a few days later, as he shakes with emotion and fights back sobs.

Bill never makes any marriage proposal as he's no fool and, despite her relish of their time together in Paris, sees no hint of a desire for a more permanent connection.

"It was hard fate that brought along the war, which caused you to cancel your holiday in Europe and our chance of meeting," he writes in 1939.

In any case, they never meet again, and all we have are Bill's letters.

"You are a DREADFUL woman!" he writes in one of them. "PLEASE [underlined three times] write and say you are receiving my odd notes written in all sorts of queer places because I have no other way of confirming the address I wrote hurriedly in my notebook and may have copied the numbers wrongly. In fact, you have been so naughty that I feel only a cable 'address correct, I do not dislike you' would earn you the honor of being permitted to appear from behind the goat hair partition of a Bedouin tent. So for the love of God, relax. Now think of all the things that are good for you. Think of camel bells, cyclamen, is that better? Now stick your chewing gum under the edge of the table—lower your bottom lip and stretch it with determination (I have only seen you do it once but it means something) and do whatever you feel the urge to do—whether a letter or a cable."

Seventy-five years later the letter still lived in Dorle's wooden chest, the address having not been the issue.

The Hotel near the Gare du Nord

My father is dead now. I can no longer ask him about Dorle's policeman, but some creaky cavity of my brain contains a story of that shipboard romance, one of several quaint anecdotes about her love life before her marriage.

Not until I began to have an affair or two of my own (dorm rooms not ship cabins, cafeterias not cafés) did I begin to understand Dorle's early loves not as stylized encounters from some sexless ancient era but matters of flesh and blood.

Years later, while poring over Dorle's love letters, I started to illustrate them in my mind.

In my few visits to Paris, I've gotten some slight sense of the changes in landscape. Not the iconic monuments so much, the Notre Dame fire aside, but the types of cheaper hotels that I could afford. I have no knowledge of the Paris pensions of the 1930s, but when I think about Dorle's meeting with Bill, one from the 1930s appears in my mind as if I'd seen their names scrawled on one of its walls.

In 1994, the 50th anniversary of D-Day, while beginning to recover from a tricky moment in our early relationship, Angela and I stayed in a place near the Gare du Nord with creaky staircases and cavernous rooms. In a cramped breakfast nook on the second floor, we met two aging Romanian semioticians who, noting our American voices, repeated "Omaha, bloody Omaha," whenever we met in the hallways.

As teens perhaps, their first visit to Paris, they could have passed Dorle and Bill in those same hallways.

Dorle dreamed up dramatic scenes for Casanova, for Parnell, for Paul Gauguin, but they are hard to find in the communications from her lovers that she'd hidden in her apartment.

While stuck in subway tunnels, biking down Brooklyn streets, showering, brushing my teeth, I've tried to summon my inner Dorle, the memories of her voice, her cigarettes, her stories. But those days in Paris are my only flight of fancy where Dorle and Bill were concerned. All that's left are his last letters distant and sad though they were.

The Arab Winter

Most of Bill's letters to Dorle were written during the chaotic Arab Revolts, which happened in Mandate Palestine during the mid- to late-1930s. British interests were self-serving at best, and their actions often cruel, but Bill's letters and "snaps" to Dorle suggest that he genuinely cared about the people for whom he had been made responsible. Gentle and sincere-sounding, Bill respected Palestinian culture enough to learn to read and write Arabic and even quoted the first line of the Koran in Arabic script. He saw himself as maintaining order rather than imposing it, and he never said anything about either Arabs or Jews that seemed racist.

"The wealthy Arabs are going or have gone to Europe or Lebanon for safety," he writes, "and the situation is steadily becoming worse … But it is my job to do my best to cope with it. I have no other training and wish for none."

Bill encloses "snaps" he takes of Palestinian life, pictures of "natives" and camels and soldiers in formation. One photo shows General Montgomery inspecting the troops, another Abdullah, the Emir of Transjordan and grandfather of the present king of Jordan, on his coronation parade.

Along with Barker's photos and letters were peculiar Christmas cards. Each was a booklet, four pages long. On the cover, there was a small piece of cloth fashioned like a bowtie with the British crown on top. Inside were sentimental watercolor images of police on the job. In one of them, two officers ride horses on a picturesque ridge. The words, "Patrol over the Judean desert," were printed below. On each card, Bill simply signed his name.

Mrs. Soria

In 1939, several years after their first encounter, just as the war is beginning, he writes the following short letter.

> *Thank you for your card and note at Christmas. It is a bit dog-eared now because I always carry a letter in my pocket until I answer it. The cyclamen came early this year. They are giving way now to summer flowers. The situation seems to go from bad to bloody awful but actually is, I suppose, no worse and it is merely tiresome trying to foresee what the future holds for us. It seems to me that whatever it is it is bound to present the police with a splitting headache, and so I think it wisest not to think about it and simply live one day at a time.*
>
> *Spare a thought for your old shipmate and try to write 'hello' occasionally.*
>
> *Yours aye,*
> *Bill*

By calling himself an "old shipmate," he has gracefully demoted himself to a regular member of the forgotten merry quartet as if those passionate nights have been blown away by time.

Bill continues to write Dorle after her marriage, addressing her as "Mrs. Soria," the "Mrs." compounding the "Soria," as indication of how far they've gone since the Lloyd Triestino journey.

Falling in love with the place you occupy may not relieve you of the burden of colonialism, but it still chokes me up to read Bill tell Mrs. Soria that he has to leave the Middle East.

"Just to say I have my bow and after ninety days I hand in my guns and seek peace. I have been invalided out of the service."

The bottom corner of the last letter did not make it to the 21st century, the partially shredded document becoming an elliptical poem about the desert Bill so desperately wanted to share with Dorle.

"It will seem strange to be committed to a world where time is calculated by mechanical means and dawn, the signal for the day to start, is not seen and sunset the time to turn over and sleep on a well-filled stomach is not noticed, except by those charged with running on lights. Where women are blatantly seen and even heard.

People who have never breathed the desert.

Not the smell of burning camel dung.

To live where horses are beasts of burden

And the camel is not known.

Where water is to bathe in.

And the body is exposed to the sun.

Where hospitality is frozen and the sheep is killed before the arrival of the guest.

And the sound of coffee pounding is not heard nor is roasting smelled.

Where today is more important than tomorrow.

And Allah's name is rarely spoken.

I am looking for a patch of sand on which to pitch a black tent, some well-bred goats and fat-raised sheep and a few women and men.

CHAPTER THREE
NAZIS, FASCISTS, AND JEWS

The Bank Building

Not a particularly curious child, I knew my maternal grandparents were born in Habsburg Prague, but I never questioned why they, as old people, would wake up at the crack of dawn in their small apartment and walk downstairs to work all day at their Cleveland bakery, whereas my Grandmother Faie and Dorle, American-born Jews, had made a lot of money and retired. I didn't realize how unusual it was for turn-of-the-last century Orthodox women to travel around the world and have professional careers rather than tend to their families. I also didn't question why Grand, their mother, got talked about in glowing terms while their father was never discussed. Growing up with one secular Jewish and one gentile parent in the very Christian Charlottesville of the 1970s, I only really became interested in my Jewish family story when Angela grew fascinated by it. All I understood about the family surname was that Jarmel, Dorle and Faie's maiden name, had somehow been derived from it. But one afternoon when I was about thirty, questions got unexpectedly answered, questions I hadn't thought to ask.

Around 1994, Angela and I were walking down Canal Street in Chinatown when she noticed a tall neo-classical building. Inside was probably a sweatshop, but ornately displayed on its facade was a bank insignia, S. Jarmulowsky and Sons. Angela grasped before I did that it had once belonged to my family.

Back home in Brooklyn, we looked it up in the *American Institute of Architecture (AIA) Guide to New York* that we happened to have on our bookshelf and learned of a crucial episode in American Jewish history that Jewish historians for generations sought to exclude. Because of a tendency towards what historian Tony Michels called "uncritical triumphalism," they wanted to erase the shameful story of the Jarmulowsky bank failure.

Nearly a century before Dorle's death, twenty-odd years before she met her master lovers on ships and at parties, a mob of poor angry Jews from the Lower East Side who had lost their savings at her family bank, surrounded her upper Manhattan apartment building, and rioted. When I learned the bare outline of an essential family story that neither my parents nor I knew anything about, I screwed up my courage and asked Dorle herself over drinks one Friday evening soon after Angela's discovery. I didn't want to traumatize her with bad memories, but I really wanted to know.

I took the subway in from Brooklyn. Upon my arrival at her Midtown apartment, we went through our rituals. I rang the bell. She opened the door, and I kissed her on both cheeks, inhaling the familiar odors of perfume, mothballs, and rotten teeth.

I poured her drink, Bombay gin and tonic. I

pulled a cigarette out of her latest pack of Benson & Hedges, handed it to her, and lit it with a match from one of the matchbooks she always took from restaurants.

Then she turned to me expectantly. It was up to me to start our conversation. Rather than request a story from her glittery past, I hesitantly broached the topic of the bank, but, as I tended to mumble when nervous and she was quite deaf, she didn't understand. Then I asked her again baldly, crassly, "Did your family have a bank? Did that bank go under?"

Had anyone mentioned the bank crash to her since the 1930s, 1920s, 1910s? Her sister, my grandmother, who had been through it with her, had died a few years before.

Dorle's eyes flipped away from me, out the window and back into the past. But when she started to speak, she sounded eager, almost child-like, like the memory had brought back her adolescence. She relived the story in quick staccato tones. I saw young Dorle and even younger Faie, my grandmother—their ingenuous faces imprinted by worry—flinging on coats, putting on boots, grabbing hold of the iron fire escape, and following my dour great-grandfather and teary-eyed great-grandmother upwards as they climbed from landing to landing. I didn't ask for more details, but S. Jarmulowsky had been Dorle's grandfather.

Dorle looked exhausted, spent, and we spoke of easier things. We asked about it just once more, Angela did, a month or so later. Dorle told us how the collapse of the bank had changed everything. They no longer kept kosher. She and my grandmother were no longer expected to have their marriages arranged. Probably, they were pariahs, other affluent Jewish families no longer considering them proper bride material. The bank crash had liberated Dorle and Faie from many of the expectations of their religion and their gender.

Using the proposal to landmark the Jarmulowsky Bank and the writings of historian, Rebecca Kobrin, whom I also interviewed, I was able to piece together the family story that Dorle had just confirmed.

What I learned about my great-great-grandfather's history inspires me, but what happened once the family got involved in New York real estate, is shameful, uncomfortable to think about over a century later.

We came from Grajewo, a Lithuanian town in the Pale of Settlement, the segment of the Russian Empire in which Jews were allowed to live.

Alexander ("Sender") Jarmulowsky, Dorle's grandfather, was born there in 1841 and was orphaned three years later after his parents died during a cholera epidemic.

When no other family members wanted the child, he was adopted by a local rabbi, and his story takes on a mythic feel, Jewish Horatio Alger. Sender quickly became so prodigious a student of the Talmud that he was ordained as a rabbi himself at an early age. And as rabbis brought both money and status to families, a marriage was soon arranged for him with Rebecca Markels, the daughter of a rich businessman.

Allowed to leave the Pale of Settlement in 1868, he and Rebecca moved to Hamburg. Once there, he devoted himself to a more lucrative field than the Talmud: providing transport to Jews leaving eastern Europe for the United States. He brokered the steerage-class boat tickets to New York so essential to the growth of the Lower East Side, which would become the largest community of Jews in the world.

Sender gained the trust of his clients by working in his rabbinical robes, as well as translating the incomprehensible German transport documents into Yiddish and Russian, so his clients could understand them. Sender would buy cheaper passages during winter with fake passenger names, then sell them for three or four times as much when the prices rose in the summer because the shipping lines were willing to change the name of passengers on tickets.

Despite his lucrative trade, Sender's application for permanent residency in Hamburg was (like most Eastern European Jews who applied, according to Kobrin) denied. That denial brought my great-great-grandfather and my great-grandfather, Louis, then just a boy, and the rest of their family to New York in 1873. The United States of that era was kinder, at least to moneyed Jews. I found Sender's American naturalization papers from 1884 among Dorle's documents.

Sender set up an office at the corner of Orchard and Canal and enlarged his business by allowing Jews already in the Lower East Side to pay installments on steerage tickets to bring other members of their family from Europe.

Sender quickly broadened the business still further to include taking deposits, giving out loans, and buying and selling foreign currency. His business had morphed into one of the largest of the immigrant banks popular at that time that were free agents within their (Jewish, Italian, Slovenian ...) communities. Unbound by federal banking regulations, they relied on personal relationships between bankers and their depositors. A figure known throughout both New York and the Pale of Settlement, Sender brought nearly half the population of the Jewish Lower East Side from Europe.

Sender substantiated the Yiddish newspaper *Morgan Zhurnal*'s contention that he was, "living proof that in America one can be a rich businessman but also a pious Jew," by overseeing and partially funding the construction of the Eldridge Street Synagogue in 1887. Built in the Moorish-revival style typical of some American synagogues of that era, it has an imposing 70-foot vaulted ceiling and church-like stained-glass windows. Which were not the German gentile builders going rogue, speculated Brad Shaw, the manager of the Eldridge Street Museum, but typical of synagogue architecture as the architects were copying the Christian trappings of American houses of worship. The Central Synagogue in Midtown built a few decades earlier, has similar windows.

After President Coolidge limited Jewish immigration from eastern Europe in the 1920s and many worshippers left for Brooklyn and other greener pastures, the congregation dwindled, and the building fell into disrepair. The few congregants worshipped in the bottom level, while the temple upstairs became ankle deep in pigeon excrement.

In the last twenty years, it has been immaculately preserved though the enormous, stunning rose window is an original design by Kiki Smith.

But before the completion of the synagogue, the North Atlantic Passenger Conference's 1896 decision to fix shipping fares spelled trouble for the Jarmulowsky business.

They supplemented their income by getting involved in real estate. Sender had already acquired buildings after clients defaulted on loans. But it was really his son Meyer, Sender's likely successor, who became the most successful *realestatenik*. Rather than the crowded Lower East Side, Meyer concentrated on Harlem. By 1912, he owned more than twenty buildings there.

After Louis and Meyer took money from depositors to buy dozens of buildings in Harlem, they became involved in redistricting Black neighborhoods so that members of those communities could not receive housing loans—early redlining.

Like some terrible Jewish character too broad and obvious for an early Spike Lee Joint, Meyer spoke at St. Philip's, an important Black church at that time, about "The Housing Problem from the Owner's Point of View," claiming that redlining was about Black people's failure to keep up their property and suggesting that Black people learn from the Jews and purchase buildings, even though he was actively trying to prevent that from happening, as well as ignoring economic disparity and racism, his actions a Trumpian cocktail of real estate, lies, racism, and New York.

The Jarmulowskys' next claims to infamy were the precedents set by lawsuits lost against them.

In one of these, Sender had paid contractors to fix faulty fire escapes in his buildings, but one fell and crippled a toddler. The ensuing suit lost against him established the dangerous precedent that lasted until the middle of the twentieth century that property owners were not liable for personal injury in their buildings unless it could be proven that they had prior knowledge of the problems that caused the injury.

In 1912, Sender contracted a building that Kobrin calls another "kind of temple for the Lower East Side," so Jews "could worship their new American God, Capitalism."

The clock in the carved panel above the corner entrance to the Jarmulowsky Bank is gone, but the helmeted figure of Hermes, the god of trade and travel, remains.

Nine Orchards, a boutique hotel with several bars, opened in the spot in the summer of 2022, but Hermes remains, heralding Sender's dual role as banker and seller of steerage tickets to Jews seeking to reach the new world.

The family bank building that Angela had

spotted was designed by Rouse and Goldstone, a popular architecture firm of the time. At twelve stories, the "Jewish Temple of Finance," as it was known, loomed over the Lower East Side.

Sender died just before his bank building opened in 1912, and the estate of a man assumed to be a multimillionaire turned out to be only $500,000. Most of the money had been spent buying 37 buildings in East Harlem.

The death of Archduke Ferdinand two years later signaled the beginning of the end for the Jarmulowskys' power and reputation and a disaster for thousands of Lower East Side Jews.

Worried about the possibility of war in Europe, many depositors withdrew money from the Jarmulowsky bank to send to relatives overseas.

"Black Tuesday" was described by Irving Howe in *World of Our Fathers*: "The outbreak of the war...led many Jewish investors to withdraw their money, partly out of the general sense of alarm, and partly because they wanted to send help to relatives trapped in Europe."

According to Kobrin, they had only $654,000 available dollars and owed more than 1.73 million, so the money quickly ran out.

The bank disaster was comically foretold ten years before it happened in David Warfield's 1904 portrait of Lower East Side life, *Ghetto Silhouettes*. A sleazy trio, "Weinberg, the sweatshop man, Einstein, the dealer in buttons and tailor's trimmings, and Weinhole, the petticoat maker," conspire to profit from a false run on the "Jobbleousky" (a fictionalized Jarmulowsky) bank, which ends up working out entirely in the noble Jobbleousky's favor. "You saved me $20,000 in interest, which is, of course, clear profit, and made about $5,000 yourselves," Jobbleousky announces after foiling them. "But if you will kindly bring in your passbooks, I shall close your accounts for good. Tomorrow morning, I have the honor to inform all three of you, you will be arrested on a charge of malicious conspiracy, for which you were indicted yesterday."

While Jobbelousky had been righteous and heroic, the reputation of his namesake, Jarmulowsky, was surely marred by the bank collapse that happened a couple of years after his death.

The depositors began to riot.

They encircled the bank.

"Let us go over to the Jarmulowsky's and make those thieves tell us when they will give us our money," the *New York Times* had quoted a "soap box orator" at a demonstration in front of the bank.

They surrounded Meyer's house. They surrounded my great-grandfather Louis's, where Dorle and the rest of her family escaped to the roof.

Meyer held a meeting with the depositors and agreed to pay 15 pennies on every dollar, then ten more pennies for the following six years.

But the depositors were far from satisfied. The *New York Tribune* describes what happened. An angry man, "fury blazing from his eyes," broke his way through the crowd and approached Meyer. Then "made a prodigious leap, snatched a weapon from his pocket. Before the startled banker could raise an arm to guard his life, a keen blade was on his throat."

Fortunately, Sulzer, the family lawyer, somehow stopped him. Otherwise, Meyer's "life blood would have spotted the carpet."

The Jarmulowsky failure led to the creation of banking laws for private banks that ushered out the era of the immigrant bank.

Though the Jarmulowskys' were rumored to be worth two million dollars in 1918, the sale of their properties garnered less than $400,000, all of which was owed the depositors.

Meyer Jarmulowsky changed his name to Jarmuth and became an architect. "By 1961," Kobrin concludes her discussion of my family, "almost all of the remaining descendants had changed their names, perhaps to escape the stain of their family's failure."

Which was true, of course, of Dorle Jarmel, though Kobrin had not heard of her.

The family bank scandal did not strip Dorle, Faie, and their mother of all their wealth, but the Orthodox traditions that would have limited them were more or less abandoned.

Dorle had no children and neither of Faie's two children, my father and Jill, nor their children, myself included, ever really looked back. I may never have learned my family story if the bank building hadn't stared Angela in the face. If it were not for the bank and its ignominious collapse, there may well have been *Master Lovers* (nothing could restrain Dorle's imagination), but probably no actual lovers as Dorle would probably have been married off young and procreated appropriately.

A few years after the bank went under, Dorle, Grand, Faie, and Mrs. Gershwin, Ira and George's mother, took off for a long European sojourn. A new life had been launched, one that would bring Dorle into the orbit of Toscanini, Hemingway, and ultimately her husband, Dario.

Bringing Hitlerism Here

Infuriated by the press coverage of the bank scandal, Dorle's father, Louis, had been incensed when Dorle wanted to take a journalism class. But upon Dorle's return to America from Europe after her father's fall from grace, she became one of the first women to attend Columbia School of Journalism.

She'd only worked briefly as a journalist when she met Arthur Judson. A talented but unexceptional musician ("I was a good violinist, but no Kreisler or Heifetz"), Judson had strategically moved from performance into management. By the early thirties, Concert Management Arthur Judson, Inc. had morphed into Columbia Artists Management, the company that would manage most American classical muscians, including those of the New York Philharmonic.

By the beginning of the 1930s—the era of the first letters from John Carter—Dorle was in her early thirties, unmarried and working with Toscanini and the New York Philharmonic, and her sister, Faie, was giving birth to my father.

When I described John's letters to my father soon after finding them, he went through the list of Dorle's lovers before her marriage, the ones she told stories about. There was the Kipling-nicknamed Mowgli, a classmate of Dorle's at the Columbia School of Journalism, who accused her of being a *"demi vierge,"* half virgin, when she wouldn't go all the way. José Iturbi, the Spanish musician, got his friend Diego Rivera to make her a sketch, which she gave me on my thirtieth birthday. Probably the one she talked most about, though, was Georges Asfar, the Syrian antiquities dealer.

But my father had never heard of John Franklin Carter though he'd written Dorle hundreds of dramatic letters over a course of five years.

Soon after discovering the Carter letters, I had found basic information about Carter in his obituary and short Wikipedia entry: journalist, FDR, etc. Carter was best known for his popular column about the New Deal in *Liberty Magazine* under the name, Jay Franklin. In 1941, *Time Magazine* called him the "New Deal's most doctrinaire supporter." A more recent *Time* story explained that he was also one of several spies personally recruited by the president during the war.

When I looked up Carter's name in the *New York Times* archive, I expected to discover more about himself and Roosevelt, but an alarming article emerged.

Not only had Dorle's father been partially

responsible for one of the darker days in New York Jewish history, Dorle's great lover from the 1930s appeared to have had Nazi associations.

"To Bring Hitlerism Here," read the heading of the 1932 story, "John Carter Named in Berlin to Head Organizing of New Party."

"Mr. Carter's appointment was revealed today," the article explained, "when he gave out an interview accorded him in his capacity by Hermann Goering, the National Socialist Chairman of the now defunct Reichstag."

Dorle's future lover had apparently been deputized by Goering to start a "Hitlerist" party to run in the 1932 election. Right before his Roosevelt days, John—-to steal Sarah Palin's phrase from the 2008 election—"was palling around with terrorists." It was after seeing Goering that Carter first met Dorle on the *Île de France* sailing from France to New York.

Though she'd confided in her adolescent diary that she thought that she had "gotten beyond the state during which I worshiped an old gentleman with whiskers," she contributed to the Spanish and Portuguese Synagogue in the Upper West Side as an adult and buried her mother, husband, and sister in an Orthodox Jewish cemetery far out in Queens. Could she really have abided a man running for president against her beloved Roosevelt on an anti-Semitic platform?

I felt dazed, jumbled. Aunt Dorle had been a hair's breadth away from a history I'd never known existed. Apparently, Putin was not the first fascist to try to influence an American election. A man selected by one of Hitler's key henchmen to run against Roosevelt had seduced my suddenly inexplicable great-aunt.

How she loved powerful men! I thought of her *Master Lovers* depiction of Henry VIII: "no monster but a powerful generous man with golden hair and beard, penetrating blue eyes and a ruddy face." A few years before her future husband would come from Italy to escape the Holocaust, Dorle had apparently been in love with a Nazi-sympathizer. If I'd looked harder in her apartment, would I have discovered another volume of *Master Lovers* featuring Hitler, Franco, Mussolini? If she'd lived further into the century, we might have read about Donald J. Trump of the magnificent orange hair urging his followers to take off their masks and take over Congress before bathing in the nude with his dozens of doting porn stars.

Back in Virginia, my mother was dying, but, wild-eyed, I carried on to anyone who would listen about my great-aunt and her married "Hitlerist" lover, spending my mother's last months back in the thirties, the decade of her childhood.

It no longer surprised me so much that Dorle could have been so close with the Nazi sympathizers who dominated the music world after the war, like Elizabeth Schwarzkopf, Goebbel's star soprano and probable mistress, and Wagner's descendants, Wieland and Winifred. When I think of Dorle's Judaism, I see her and her family climbing up to the roof to escape a mob of angry Jews as if she were still running from them years later or, more metaphorically from a sense of Jewish identity.

A few months after my discovery of Carter's "Hitlerism," I finally (clumsily) began to dig around for more information about it. But aside from the stunning story about Carter and Goering, news stories about him hardly mentioned it. There is only one other reference to his party in the 1932 elections. The *North Adams Transcript,* his hometown paper, claimed he had formed it after being fired from the Hoover State Department for writing columns critical of Hoover under a pen name, but said nothing about Hitlerism. Goering's ostensible endorsement didn't stop Roosevelt from enlisting Carter as a New Dealer and later tasking him with espionage. The Hitlerist accusation got harder and harder to figure.

Not a proper researcher sifting through archives, I acted like an amateur fisherman randomly setting up rods.

Convinced that Carter was too minor a figure to have archives, I allowed nearly a year to pass before stumbling upon their existence in Cheyenne at the University of Wyoming. I was busily planning what felt like an epic and exotic journey westward when the archive offered to scan everything relevant for a fraction of the cost.

Amidst the material sent to me, I came across a letter Carter wrote to The *New Republic* in 1937 that solved some of the mystery of his Hitlerist party and their quixotic run against FDR. Responding to I.F. Stone's claim (in a blistering review of Carter's biography of Fiorello La Guardia) that he had "swung all the way from sympathy with Nazism to New Dealism," Carter asserted that his party, not at all Hitlerist, was actually encouraged by Roosevelt so that "conscience-stricken conservatives could embark on liberal policies," thereby siphoning off the Republican vote and paving the way for FDR.

Carter explained that Eduard Heriot, the French prime minister, had sent him to Germany to "ascertain the future policy of the Nazis," and Fredrick Birchall of the *New York Times* had asked him to interview Hitler while there. The future führer proving unavailable, he had met with Goering instead. Carter claimed that he had sent the ensuing interview to Birchall only to find it "materially altered," that shocking article about Carter that I'd found in the *Times*.

Also in the material from the John Carter archives was a document mislabeled "John Carter's diary 1932." "For Sheila," read John's dedication to what turned out to be his wife's journal, "in the hope that 1932 will be as happy as past years and more interesting than some years."

Sheila unwittingly backed up John's claim to have been a Roosevelt supporter by announcing that she and her husband "feel tired but more than happy after the election."

But I was surprised by her animated description of early Nazi Germany. On September

5, in Munich, "John sent his introduction to Ernst Hanfstaengl, Hitler's Chief of Press," who Sheila immediately refers to affectionately as "Putzi." With Putzi, they attended a "Hitler meeting, a large and enthusiastic crowd in a tightly closed building holding about 1800."

"He was accompanied," she reports, "by guards, flags, music, quite a good show."

Then "Putzi persuaded us to go to Berlin for the dissolution of the Reichstag." "All Berlin," Sheila exclaims, "feels electric over showdown in Reichstag—where all the traffic has been stopped, heavy police guards posted."

Again and again, Sheila makes the American-educated Putzi sound like a pal with whom she was in chummy accord and presents the political environment in Germany as more thrilling than threatening.

In 1937, just as Putzi was being removed from Hitler's inner circle by Goebbels, he wrote Carter a strange but friendly letter on official Reich stationery. Putzi suggested minor revisions to what he calls "that dream interview with Goering." Putzi did not seriously object to an interview that the *Times* transformed into an apology for Hitlerism, so John probably painted a favorable portrait of Goering. Goering might not have agreed to the interview if that hadn't been implicit in the deal.

Finally, Putzi requests that John and Sheila no longer refer to him as Putzi but simply as Putz, which we know (would he?) is Yiddish slang for a dickish, generally worthless person.

Where does this leave John's Hitlerism? Deputized to start a Nazi party, no, but probably sympathetic to the cause. John never mentions his trip to Berlin nor his interview with Goering to Dorle in his letters, and I can only hope he never did in person as she stayed with him for half a decade.

Dorle was a reliable big D Democrat, a great admirer of Eleanor Roosevelt, and never spoke favorably of strongmen. But the more I learned about her world in the thirties and forties, the more people I found associated with authoritarianism I found, authoritarianism in its many different flavors.

Georges Asfar's politics were the hardest to figure. The Damascus Room in the Metropolitan Museum was donated by Hagop Kevorkian but originally sold by Georges. Mecka Baumeister, a conservator involved in the restoration of the room, told me he'd ripped entire rooms from nineteenth-century Ottoman homes in Damascus and sent them around the western world.

Georges hated Muslim Arabs (particularly Palestinians) and feared Syrian independence as if he were some native (actually Syrian) species of colonialist.

Bill Barker, bona fide colonialist, may have spent the thirties trying to stop Jews and Arabs from killing each other, but in the role of a British occupier. And just a decade before was when he'd been a Black and Tan in Ireland. A friend from

Dublin told me an ominous family story dating from Barker's time in Ireland of his grandmother as a young girl hearing a Black and Tan vehicle approach and "running into the middle of the field and hiding in the long grass, shaking with fear until the truck passed."

A decade or so before Dario fled the Holocaust to the United States, he'd served as an officer in the Fascist army in Eritrea. Beautifully assembled photo albums from the late twenties show him relaxing with his officer buddies in Asmara, but they treated the Africans they colonized far less elegantly. Approximately 7 percent of all Ethiopians and Eritreans were murdered by the Italians during their conquest, including nearly half a million burned and suffocated by chemical weapons during Mussolini's siege of Addis Ababa.

In one photo, the young Dario, sandy-haired years before I knew him, smiles his familiar wide smile. Dorle's ultimate master lover, the man with whom she would spend much of her life, crouches gleefully over a cheetah he has just killed.

Dorle's sister's ex-husband, my grandfather Percy (also Jewish), had been a devoted Italian fascist until late in the twenties when he accused Mussolini not of murder (the many slain partisans) but what he called "middle-classism."

Toscanini, with whom Dorle had a passionate connection if not an actual affair, was also a Fascist until he and Mussolini turned against each other.

Not fascist or authoritarian, perhaps, but her

father and uncle Meyer's redlining was insidious and malign.

Decades before I discovered Dorle's love letters, I had been shocked to learn that Angela's father, Angelo, who grew up in Italy and served in the Italian navy during the war, still believed some of Mussolini's ideas, the propaganda of his youth. Now, when I think of Dorle, my grandfather, etc., I see fascism as part of my own lineage every bit as much as it might be part of hers.

My spine shivers as I consider how easily Dorle countenanced the cruel way that both her fictional and real lovers mastered their worlds. Dazzled by the dashing figures cut by her lovers, Dorle didn't seem bothered by the humans and wildlife they may have assassinated.

Dorle's fairy-tale world was rife with moral ambiguity. From Germany to Italy to the French and British empires, axes of genuine evil were as ubiquitous as culture and romance, and Dorle breathed in as much as she could, grateful for the freedom that the demise of the family bank had brought her. The loyalty she felt for her scandal-plagued father probably prevented her from judging too harshly, and I just can't imagine her much interested in men without dark and complicated pasts in that dark and complicated decade.

CHAPTER FOUR
AN AFTERNOON WITH FATHER

Nearly a year after the sale of what had been Dorle's apartment, I discovered Dorle's childhood diary from 1916, when she herself had also been sixteen, in one of the plastic bins in which I had put her documents. The precious little notebook, nearly a century old, crumbled when I touched it.

But delivered me its secrets in neat schoolgirl script.

Much later in life, Dorle poo-poohed the struggles of working women, but her father's attitude towards her ambitions had to have stung.

When her father, Louis, became enraged because she wanted to take a journalism class, he "commenced to rant and roar" against the field, calling it "unfeminine, nihilistic, socialistic, anarchistic, radical and a great many more epithets."

The family banking crisis weighed heavy on him.

"Papa is all broken up," Dorle writes a few weeks after the journalism class debacle. "He walks around hardly knowing what he's saying —utterly crushed by the troubled financial situation."

At a family dinner, Louis cried out, "I've battled and battled," then stopped talking, his eyes welling with tears. A few weeks later, "Papa left home today for an indefinite period of time— for a few weeks, at any rate. At which I became upset and then and there had a little weep."

He had gone to Tulsa to try to make some money in the oil industry. My German Orthodox Jewish great-grandfather may not have fit so well in the roughneck world of 1917 Oklahoma. In any case, he came back empty-handed.

Late Afternoon, Fifteen Years Later: Fall, 1932

Dorle takes the side entrance to the house they purchased after the bank disaster, the entrance Father would use before he fell ill in order to avoid running into Mother.

Glimpsing the back of the dining room table, Dorle remembers those meals in the 1920s: Mother, Father, her sister Faie, and herself dining on food coming up from the kitchen on a dumbwaiter, the conversation hushed and stilted as only she would speak to her disgraced father.

The old nurse opens the door to Father's stuffy bedroom with a scowl, and Dorle smells the aroma of camphor, soap, and infirmity.

The nurse responds to Dorle's hearty "good afternoon" with an incomprehensible grumble and shows her patient's daughter to the beat-up armchair near where her patient sleeps uncomfortably.

Annoyed by the lack of basic civility, Dorle stares at the scarf on the frumpy old woman's head, a reminder of the traditional Jewish life Dorle had been lucky to escape, and frowns for a moment before composing herself and attempting a smile. Father will bear the brunt of any complaint.

After those terrible weeks in 1914—the unruly bank customers rioting in front of the house, the yelled accusations about her father and uncle that may not have been so far off the mark—Dorle understands why Mother and Faie won't speak to him. But can't they soften now that he is failing? Tears well up in Dorle's eyes as she listens to the nurse complaining to herself in Yiddish and considers the solitude Father suffers for so much of the time, the sadly unsentimental care that has been arranged for him.

Guttural sounds emerge from the bed. A deep, wet coughing fit has woken him up. Dutifully but aggressively, the nurse pounds on his back to clear his throat and wipes the mucus from his mouth.

Father's irritated eyes glimmer as he recognizes his daughter. He scratches his gray beard and blanches for a moment as if in pain before attempting to force his face into something approximating a smile.

Dorle takes his right hand, lying outside the sheets, into her own as delicately as she can as he bruises so easily now. Then plants a kiss on his haggard cheeks, her body reverberating for a moment as she recognizes his familiarly musky smell, persistent even in his dying.

His hand tugs back with as much strength as it can muster, and his eyes sparkle just a bit as he tries to focus upon his daughter.

Father tries to clear his throat, as there is something he wishes to say, but his words get stuck inside his phlegmy chest. Giving up on speaking, he groans, pulls his hand away from Dorle and knocks himself on the head.

He no longer blames the bank failure on the socialists, the anarchists, the terrible newspapers, and generally miserable populace. His own mistakes had ruined his family. His brothers and he should never have taken those funds to buy buildings in the north of the island. Replenishing them later would have been easy but for the war in Europe and the customers coming in droves to withdraw money to send to their relatives. On and on until no money was left, and the bank was forced to close.

Soon he is coughing again, the frustration stuck in his lungs.

Sternly, the nurse looks at Dorle and shakes her head. She needs no words to convey her two basic messages. It is time for Dorle to leave as her visit is straining her father and, strain or no strain, he has little more time in this world.

After kissing Father once more on his paper-thin cheeks, she flees the room, stopping briefly to glare at the nurse on the way out.

It doesn't matter how critical Father had been, how belligerent when his moods descended. It doesn't matter that the family misfortune may have been due, in part, to his mistakes. She'd jumped on his shoulders and ridden him around the house as a child and spent hours walking around Central Park with him as a teen. And he's always provided for the family, even after the bank troubles. Surely, he deserves kinder care.

But the nurse has been recommended by Rabbi Gershowitz, and Mother will never consent to replace her.

Outside on the avenue, Dorle's legs do not take her on their accustomed path uptown towards her apartment, but southward instead towards an unlikely destination that only becomes clear after several briskly paced blocks.

She strides east now, in the general direction of Canal Street, towards the bank building sold a decade before.

A few blocks farther, she crosses Houston onto the Bowery. The smells remind her before the sights and sounds: the sweat, the pee, the sharp stink of cheap spirits.

Always an unpleasant part of town, legendarily so, but so much worse since 1929, or so Dorle has heard. It is far from her usual stomping ground.

The men and the occasional women laze on stoops, drinking their spirits, munching stale bread and rotting fruit. Some just stand languidly about or sleep on piles of old newspapers on the sidewalk.

In and around them, children hold out their filthy hands and beg for coins. And listless ancients, some older than Father, stare vacantly at passersby.

In the nearest store, an unpleasant Italian

with an unkempt moustache lets Dorle buy out his meager supply of apples and loaves of bread.

The heavy bundle grows lighter as she begins to distribute her alms, placing fruit into hands, breaking loaves into smaller bits to provide nourishment to more misbegotten souls.

Who jostle each other and express no gratitude.

She circumnavigates as best she can the loutish men who probably (if Mother were to be believed) would exchange their very souls to feed their dark habit.

Which is an odd thought for Dorle to find in her mind as she enjoys a drink herself: the exuberance it achieves, evening cocktails with her friends.

But in such sharply different surroundings: those French and Italian restaurants in her neighborhood, the bars at the opera or the philharmonic during intermissions, her pleasantly spacious 57th Street apartment with a fellow over.

A grubby-faced urchin approaches with tears in her eyes soon after the last of Dorle's bounty has been distributed, and Dorle reaches into her pocket for a coin and gazes more carefully at the scene surrounding her.

Which resembles in a certain way the souks she'd recently seen in Damascus.

Because everything is for sale: shoes, torn pants and shirts, broken down pots and pans that came from their kitchens in better times. Torpidly, they list the nickels and pennies they wish to charge, but no one is buying.

And rather than exotic Arabic robes, they

wear filthy American clothes. Dorle catches the eye of an old man selling chipped dinner plates, hears his wrenching cough that reminds her of Father's and takes herself to task for the errors in her thinking. Mother felt these creatures brought about their own troubles, but Mother was wrong to hold them responsible for what fate had sent their way. Dorle thinks of Maestro conducting concerts that no one here can near afford, of her friends in the latest from Bonwit's and Bloomingdale's, of her own expensive ocean voyages and demands of herself more compassion.

Soon, she makes her way to Canal Street itself, pushing through the throngs to get closer to the grandiose façade of the bank. While gazing up at the Jarmulowsky name still prominently displayed and thinking of all she has encountered on her long walk that afternoon, she remembers John Carter, the man she'd recently met on ship who'd spoken so stirringly of the ills overtaking the country and his ambitious plans to right them.

Mild-mannered, less than handsome and a species of bureaucrat despite his elevated ambitions, John would hardly merit the company of Gaugin, Goethe, or Geoffrey Rudel, Dorle's troubadour and "pilgrim of love." But the man's talent for romantic prose nearly equaled her own. "Fly high, darling," he would write her towards the end of their affair, "and I see the top of the clouds—they're all over—use the moon for a boat and follow any star you like. But the last you shall know as I know that for us there is only one sun whose glory fills the heavens."

CHAPTER FIVE
THE HITLERIST

Part One

The *Île de France*

Gamine in her early thirties, Dorle ably climbs the spiral staircase of the *Île de France* towards the funnels at the top of the ship just ahead of the man she has recently met. Her white linen dress sparkles though her belt feels uncomfortable against a stomach swollen from recent French, Italian, and Austrian meals.

If she trips on the narrow stairs and tumbles backward, John Franklin Carter can easily catch her, but she suspects he enjoys the feel of the small of her back against his fingertips.

She'd noticed him peering at her from a distance several times during the first two days of the journey to New York, but he'd finally approached her just that afternoon while she was smoking cigarettes at the bar and perusing the telegrams that had arrived from Maestro.

What she feels tempted to rub in – as she reaches the deck near the funnels well ahead of him—is how little she requires his help. She has linered across the ocean many times, and his grayish pallor and sweaty forehead suggest a weaker constitution.

She looks over at the waves dancing in the

skyline, glances at him catching his breath and regaining his composure, and wonders why she finds him appealing with his small eyes and feminine lips. Iturbi, her last lover, was so much more handsome but could be so elusive, detached.

And once Carter had caught Dorle's eyes, he'd locked on to them like all else had vanished.

He looks disgruntled now, though, as the sliver of moon he had wanted to show her, peculiarly luminescent from their perch near the funnels, has been covered in clouds.

But a moment later, it emerges over the shimmering ocean, and Dorle breathes deeply in polite appreciation.

Pleased by the success of their adventure, he returns to his favorite topic, the political party he has founded in America that will run in the upcoming 1932 elections. They believe in the commitment of the individual to society, the prevention of big business from robbing people blind, and the restoration of national pride that the Depression has drained from common Americans.

And Dorle has seen the food lines and the beggars, the grinding poverty eating up the outer reaches of the city. And has been puzzled by tremendous changes afoot in Europe. Her focus on Toscanini and the Philharmonic, as inspiring as it's been, has taken her away from the struggles surrounding her, the political questions of the day. Here was a man addressing those very concerns, a man doing something important in the world.

Her young face sparkles, but her Semitic cheekbones make Carter uneasy. He must never bring up the topic of Germany, Goering, and that misbegotten story in the *Times*.

Particularly not the Hitler rally that he'd recently attended with his wife that had stretched beyond his limited German comprehension except for that recognizable cognate, "*Juden!*" over and over again.

An Anglo-Saxon minister's son himself, he admires the pith and acumen of the Jewish people and has always liked their women.

When they say their goodbyes near dawn after several champagne cocktails, she allows his goodnight kiss to land nearer her lips than her cheek.

Sheila Carter: Hints of an Affair

The earliest hints of Dorle and John's affair weren't in his letters but in his wife, Sheila's, diary.

When John returns to America before she does, sailing on the *Île de France* on September 22, Sheila feels "very deserted," a strong emotion for only a few weeks of separation and a harbinger of things to come, as John may desert her for the woman he meets on board.

And in early October—after meeting Dorle on board and arriving by himself in America—John seems to consider marooning his wife in order to woo Dorle. While still in France, Sheila writes the following in her diary:

Oct 3: Sent John a cable asking if I would sail Oct 12.

Oct 5: Went to French line to reserve passages in case we can sail on the 12th.

Oct 6: Had a note from Philip about Putzi. Still no word from John feeling very discouraged.

But chooses not to.

Oct 7: Very excited about getting to sail on the 12th.

A slight, pretty woman in her early thirties with light brown hair and delicate cheekbones waits patiently at the dock in Le Havre on the line to reserve passages, wearing a modest gray dress and shivering slightly in the cold fall sun. She wonders what John could possibly be up to. Not hearing from him was unusual. Perhaps his wires had been somehow intercepted.

John Corresponds/
Love Blossoms

On September 30th, while Sheila was still in France, John composed his quite formal first letter to Dorle.
    "You may recollect that you asked me on the *Île de France* to send you some of the cards and literature of the New National Party. Naturally, both

our manifesto and plans for future action will be considered after the election when I shall send you further information," he informs her, signing off officiously, "Yours sincerely, John Franklin Carter, Chairman, Organizing Committee."

His business-like tone breaks apart a month later in his second letter, as he bewails, "his rather bleak workplace... very hard and alone and efficient."

And discusses the uncertainty of his "return" to New York revealing that he'd been there just recently.

The telephone brays like in a screwball comedy, and Dorle strolls across the large rectangular living room of her 57th Street apartment into the foyer where it's located.

The hollow silence on the other line suggests an international call and a distant British voice tells her it is Herr Armin Vogler from Bayreuth calling person to person.

He's Winifred Wagner's assistant trying to get an answer to the question Maestro has not yet been able to decide, whether he will renege on his contract to conduct at Bayreuth over the summer. He loves conducting Wagner there, but after Mussolini had turned against him and he'd been intimidated by Fascist thugs, he'd lost his stomach for that brand of politics.

After the usual pleasantries—the health of Frau Vogler, Maestro, and Dorle's mother—there is an awkward silence while Vogler launches into his preamble, the Wagner family appreciation for the brilliant Toscanini that no government could put aside.

While Herr Vogler searches for the right English word to argue that great art lay beyond the reach of politics, Dorle explains that Maestro still hasn't decided.

Tired from a long day at her office and tipsy from an after-work drink, she plays the trick she's mastered.

She moves her mouth farther and farther from the phone. "Herr Vogler," she says, "I'm afraid I'm losing you."

When the phone starts up again a few moments later, she resolves to ignore it, but on the eleventh or twelfth ring, she picks it up as she realizes that poor Armin is caught between a rock and a hard place: Maestro refusing to decide, Winifred breathing down his back. She doesn't know how she can help, but she should at least pick up the phone.

But the voice speaking her name on the other line sounds much nearer than Germany.

"Dorle," repeats the familiarly nasal New England voice, "it's John."

Dorle puzzles for a moment as she still has Armin Vogler on her mind.

"John Carter," John clarifies.

However enjoyable their shipboard flirtation, however inspiring his ambitions, it had been folly to agree to distribute pamphlets for his little party as Roosevelt, the man one really should support, was bound to win.

But her heart beats faster than it should. Her palms sweat unusually.

They'd only ever held hands and kissed each other on the cheeks, but his face had lit up each time they'd run into each other after their interlude up at the funnels, and the sadness in his eyes when they'd said their goodbyes had stuck with her all afternoon.

At that moment, Dorle wears a blue bathrobe over a white nightgown, her basic morning attire into the twenty-first century.

When he asks if they can dine the next night, she makes him wait until she checks her diary. She's booked to meet the second violinist of the Philharmonic and his dreary Flemish wife at a Hungarian restaurant on the East Side, but when she returns to the phone after confirming that in her diary, she tells him that she's free.

She really can't help the violinist with his concertmaster aspirations, and John was friends with Roosevelt. The thought of herself as the Jewish Eleanor Roosevelt passes quickly in and out of her mind; as it's really the memory of John's face that compels her, the brooding intensity of his eyes.

They eat at Le Quercy, a restaurant a few blocks south of her apartment with a bar in front, where you can wait for your date, and several evenly spaced rows of tables with waiters expertly spinning back and forth bearing silver platters.

John arrives late and frazzled. His meeting

with a potential donor had not gone well. Pausing at the vestibule of the restaurant, he straightens his tie, digs around his incisors with his tongue, and sniffs his underarms to make sure the eau de cologne has not evaporated before he rushes in.

Prettier than he had remembered, her ample bosom visible under her dress, Dorle smiles widely at him, welcomingly.

He orders a bottle of champagne and is selecting their meals, his habit when he dines with his wife, but comes to an abrupt halt after the words "escargot," as Dorle is a career woman and may want to order for herself.

Dorle takes advantage of the hesitation to request her usual fare—*sole meuniere*—and to sagely suggest that he try the *boeuf bourguignon*.

Light-headed from champagne and jittery with nerves, he rambles on about his long-term goals: governor or secretary of state as his recent European trip revealed a knack for foreign affairs.

They eat voraciously, beef and fish disappearing into their stomachs, and after they have both chosen Napoleons from the elaborate dessert cart, John finally remembers to ask Dorle the question she gets twice a day on average about working with the famously temperamental Toscanini.

Whose warmth she praises, whose humor.

She considers letting him in on the story of the brave Toscanini standing down those Fascist thugs in Milan but isn't sure she should entrust him with guarded information.

John's politics seem vague and grandiose,

and she can't get a handle on his loyalties. Italian Fascism had always seemed excessive, even when Maestro had been an adherent, just the sort of dogma that appealed to ambitious men like John.

Outside the restaurant, John grabs her by her hand and looks intently into her eyes. Subtly, she shrugs her shoulders and turns her palms to the sky to signify resignation. She will not resist. The evening does not have to end prematurely.

Later, in her apartment, she pours them brandies and sits across from him in an armchair while he perches anxiously on the couch.

Fresh out of words, he rises stiffly and stumbles towards her. Grabbing her in his arms, he presses his lips against hers until her mouth opens, and her hands grab hold of his shoulders. Matter-of-factly, she unbuttons his shirt once they've reached her bedroom and unties his tie before slipping off her dress.

Afterwards, she forgives him for lasting only minutes inside her with a wry shake of her head before modestly slipping her body deeper into the sheets. But a wary expression settles on her face as she sees him rush nervously into his clothes.

"A wife?" she wants to know.

Her words shudder through him, and he nods his head.

"In France now," he confesses, feeling for his wedding band in his breast pocket, "but she expects to wake up to my wire."

Nodding her head, Dorle waves him an abrupt goodbye and buries her head in her pillow.

This hardly surprises her. Men his age have wives. Mother might shake her head piously, but Dorle has no pressing reason to tell her.

After hearing the front door delicately close, Dorle recalls the pleasure on his face when she'd invited him up to her apartment and the grimace when he'd been forced to admit he had a wife, so different from eternally blasé Iturbi. John was dedicated to his country, profound, sincere.

Which isn't exactly true, of course. If he were truly so pure, he'd be with his wife in France, not with Dorle in New York. But he must feel too passionately about her to contain himself. He may not have looked like a Byron, a young Werther —he would have hardly merited a chapter in the lovers book she'd written when she was young— but he had that same *romantischen geist* as if born of sonnet or ballad.

And listening to him discuss her country's problems made her feel less complacent. Whenever she strayed from her opulent neighborhood, she glimpsed crowds of cold, hungry people worse off than the Jews who'd lost their money in the family bank.

Solving poverty is among John's missions. He'd discussed it so movingly.

Thoughts of him, generally pleasant ones, fill her mind as she falls asleep. They greet her when she wakes up the following morning.

A Father's Fall

When Dorle's father, Louis, dies a few weeks after Dorle and John's first sexual encounter, John coolly points out that "There is nothing that can be said in the face of death—it is a fact." Banal, not very comforting.

John, the sincere, the passionate, was temporarily shelved, leaving John, the clubfooted, the unfeeling.

To whom she vehemently responded.

After John leaves for the day one morning soon after Louis's death, Sheila scampers up the stairs to his office, wearing the flowing, salmon-colored dressing gown with an elaborate bow on which she'd splurged in hopes of recapturing John's dwindling sexual appetite. It is rumpled now as she's worn it for two nights running.

John's been behaving strangely, and she wants to see what he's been up to.

Going through the papers on his desk, she sees drafts of his latest murder mystery and documents involving the political party in which he seemed to be losing interest. She is turning around, about to descend the staircase, when her eyes happen upon a sheet of notebook paper with handwriting upon it ripped into pieces in the little trash bin near John's desk.

Her heart beats faster and her headache intensifies as she puts the pieces back together and begins to read.

"John gave me a horrible shock," she will tell her diary, "by hiding destroyed letters from a silly woman who wrote him in a wild fashion after he sent a note of sympathy on her father's death. I should say an excellent specimen for Freud."

The next day Sheila writes that "John and I had a long miserable talk and finally cleared everything up."

The End of the Party /
The Deepening of the Affair

The next time John writes Dorle, the 1932 elections are over, and the New National Party has fallen out of history. He promises to "explain his political odyssey," but there is no further reference to the party in any of his hundreds of letters to Dorle.

Except for the oblique allusion to John's flirtation with Nazism in I.F. Stone's fierce review of Carter's book about La Guardia in The *New Republic,* the whole issue seems wiped from memory.

"I miss you in so many ways," John declares in the same letter, "that there is no pretending that I don't."

That Christmas he drank heavily, sending her a message that he wasn't "resentful of anything only in a fever of sleeplessness and lack of drink." The word "lack" had been crossed out.

But even now, at the very beginning, while avidly declaring his love, John keeps his distance, reminding her and perhaps himself of his family and work obligations.

"The only line I can see clearly to follow," he will explain a couple of months later, laying down the ground rules for the affair, "is one that will satisfy no one—that I do the best I can to meet my obligations, and not come to New York except when it is natural or necessary to do so." He will only visit if business takes him there, as a trip with adultery as his sole motive plunges him into seamier moral territory. In fact, Sheila records his several trips to New York in the last months of 1932 without expressing doubt or suspicion despite her interception of that "silly woman's" letter.

Carter's moral code does not require much sacrifice on his part as his business is always bringing him to New York. The flurry of assignations only months after their shipboard encounter must have been their most passionate period.

"Half the time I feel like a chap, a cheating unscrupulous scoundrel, and the rest of the time I have wanted to give you a beating. I realize that it can be uncomfortable to be half civilized and half primitive."

John may see Dorle, an unmarried Jewess, as akin to the period view of the Black woman, more animal than wife, impulsive, difficult to tame.

After arriving in New York on an early train from Washington, he calls her and arranges to see her. He meets editors and political bosses, and at the end of the day rendezvouses with her.

They eat at Quercy, Caravelle or other nearby

French or Italian restaurants, gobble down rich meals and discuss Roosevelt, Europe, and the distant clouds of war. Then slip as unobtrusively past her doorman as possible into her apartment building.

Sheila lies quietly in her nightgown when she and John still have sex, waiting for her husband to climb diligently on top of her. But Dorle and John tear away at each other, gnawing and nibbling, spanking and yowling.

In the early days of 1933, Dorle is like a potion for John, an antidepressant. He is kinder to Sheila, warmer with his children. His columns grow more fiery, his ambitions soar.

Mood Crash

But that spring, John suffers from the first in a series of crises that will characterize his years with Dorle—bipolar-like mood swings decades before the term.

A vertiginous sensation overcomes him as he leaves Dorle's apartment late one evening. The onions from that dinner's carbonara climb the walls of his esophagus. The halls spin riotously around him though he's had no more than usual to drink. The suddenly gloomy world envelops him like a lethal cocoon as he slops through the viscous Midtown streets.

Meanwhile, he can't make it to New York and is pent up with frustration.

"I seem to be further from New York than

ever," he writes on June 20th. There had been a chance, he explains, of being called there to deliver copy, but it was sent by registered mail instead, leaving him "fairly desperate."

While in this inflamed state, he runs into trouble with his family: "a secondary crisis that in no way involves you threatens the break-up of my whole family, everything."

John tries to be collected, debonair during his evenings with Dorle.

But watch him receive the news from his editor that the manuscript is to be sent registered mail, depriving him of his excuse to go to New York. It is around noon on a day in which he has been working in the large studio atop the house on Capitol Hill that he shares with his wife, their daughter, and his two stepdaughters.

Though he has proclaimed to Dorle on several occasions how much he enjoys spending time with a modern career woman not tied to any kitchen, he storms down the stairs to demand his lunch after receiving the demolishing news.

The girls are at school, and his wife has prepared the ham sandwich with coleslaw that he generally enjoys, but the bread is stale, the ham greasy, and to top it off, they've run out of mustard.

And when it turns out they also don't have beer, the only thing in his life he feels he can look forward to, he turns to his wife again, solemnly shakes his head and demands to know why she "insisted" on "failing" him "in every imaginable department." Then he marches triumphantly out of the kitchen and dashes back to his office, slamming the door behind him.

After burying himself in his latest editorial for *Liberty Magazine,* flailing furiously away at the Republican opponents of the New Deal, he slips downstairs in search of that same ham sandwich as he's hungry and even that would suffice to find teary-eyed Sheila in their bedroom packing clothes into a suitcase. We know from her diary how fragile and sad she could be, how hard John's tantrums must have been for her. Breathing deeply, she tells him that she's taking herself and the girls to her mother's

John's anger and frustration dissipate when he sees the sadness in Sheila's puffy eyes. Her pretty face, so plaintive now, had meant absolutely everything to him since the end of the last war. His affair with Dorle would crack Sheila open if she were to learn of it.

John initiates what he knows will have to be an extended apology, pleading the "nightmarish pressure" he's been under of late, the terrible pallor cast on him by the *New York Times* hatchet job, all the work for Roosevelt, and his myriad columns. When he sees a little bending in her eyes, the possibility of returning from her mother's after a week or so in exile, he gobbles his sandwich, climbs back up the stairs to his office and begins his latest letter to Dorle.

He's asking her to visit Washington as he'll have the house to himself when his eyes stray out the window towards the back of that Republican congressman's house, and he thinks about the nosy minister who lives across the street.

He has the "wild idea," he explains to Dorle, of asking her to come visit, but his house turns out to be "surrounded by hostile neighbors of the sort who write anonymous letters, and except for the hotels facing the Union Depot, [he is] fairly well-known by most of Washington's hoteliers."

Half a Century Later

New York City, Halloween. I am twenty-four and something of a mess, working off the books moving office furniture and delivering inexplicable packages for someone in Brooklyn I met through a friend after having failed as an editorial assistant. The lease has run out in the apartment where I had been living with two college friends in the dumpy lower part of Park Slope, and I have been crashing on the couches of friends and family: my Grandmother Faie and, more recently, Dorle's. My plan is to deliver something to Long Island City, run back to meet my friends at the parade, and eventually, late in the evening, return to Dorle's to sleep.

But everything gets screwed up. It takes me too long to find the place in Long Island City, and I miss my friends. In that pre-cellular era, all I can do is head dismally back to Dorle's where I know she is out for the evening. At that point, she is nearly ninety.

Soon after my arrival, I hear a strange sound coming from just outside. Dorle, home early, is struggling with the door as I have locked it incorrectly.

I manage to let her in, but her eyes are wild and annoyed. She takes a deep breath before telling me in a clear, calm voice that she has "sad news."

My heart stops as I imagine, illogically, that something has happened to my parents in Virginia, and Dorle has somehow learned of it before I have.

"Faie died," she tells me, which makes no sense as my grandmother had seemed fine when I last saw her only days before.

Faie had been a key figure for me, the closest member of my extended family. Having lost both grandfathers young, I was certainly aware that grandmothers were likely to be the next to go, but the vital, meticulous Faie, at whose apartment I spent so many nights since moving to New York less than a year and a half before, seemed like a permanent fixture on this planet. The circumstances of her death—so simply and clearly described by Dorle just after it happened—have haunted me ever since.

Whereas Dorle grew slightly plump in old age, tiny Faie was bone thin with long hair in a jet-black ponytail that I never realized was dyed.

She and Dorle had gone to an evening film at the Museum of Modern Art cinematheque, which in the late eighties was still a small and unassuming theater down a staircase just inside from the main entrance.

Insatiably social and obsessively reliable, Faie never canceled engagements.

She did not feel right that evening. Nauseated, out of breath, but if she could make it down the old-fashioned manual elevator of her apartment building and into a cab, she would go. And she could.

On the short drive over, she felt weaker and weaker. It occurred to her to tell the cabbie to turn around and go back, but then everything would have been so complicated. Where would she have located the telephone number of the box officer of the theater? Her sister would have already left for the movie. She couldn't simply not show up. It wasn't something she did.

She makes it to the museum, takes the elevator down to the theater, and nonchalantly pecks her sister on the cheek.

Shet hardly focuses on the film as her head pounds, bile collects in her throat, and the theater begins to spin around her.

"I'm not well," she announces to Dorle, who takes her by the hand and leads her out of the theater, into the elevator, back to the street, and into a cab.

"Driver, take me to 14 East 75th Street," Dorle reports Faie's extremely characteristic last words, explaining that Faie had stayed silent the whole ride before vomiting and collapsing dead on the floor of the lobby of her building, the EMT unable to revive her.

Her old age plus Orthodox Jewish tradition precluded any autopsy, so I never learned what killed her so suddenly.

Seventy-three years earlier, sixteen-year-old

Dorle wrote that Faie "has certainly grown up fast and longs to do things I do, have boyfriends, go out a great deal, etc. I know I have failed her at times of mental and moral crisis, but truly I want to be a factor for good in her life."

Preternaturally calm in the wake of her sister's death, Dorle allows me to hug her but wriggles away, as she needs to inform my parents and begin making arrangements.

Fortune had landed me beside Dorle just moments after the death of the baby sister she'd known for 85 years.

The longer she lived, the more self-assured she may have become, but I still can't imagine someone with such sangfroid countenancing John Franklin Carter's constant melodrama.

I see Dorle using her gold letter opener to get to John's missive about Union Depot hotels. Already over thirty by that point, old for marriage and children by the standards of her day, she reads his words and feels her emotions tangle inside her.

Crushed not to see him, a tiny bit tempted to take him up on his implicit invitation to run down to Washington and make love in a seedy hotel but also infuriated by the high drama he seemed to make out of everything, which in good moments recalled her master lovers, but in bad ones seemed downright feminine.

She gets a sudden attack of the giggles as

she imagines him as secretary of state.

She'd met the French ambassador herself. A pleasant, down-to-earth, rather conservative man who'd been an attaché in Tirana during the First War.

In Dorle's imaginary scenario, it would be a perfectly normal, run of the mill consultation with John Carter until something not intended to be inflammatory gets under the skin of the secretary of state.

Brushing his hair back with his hands in that actorly way, John lets loose a florid explosion of words, difficult for the poor ambassador to understand. The puzzled man calls for a brandy. Placing his hand gently on Carter's shoulder, he watches in amazement as the weeping Secretary of State takes deep breaths and struggles to calm himself.

"The other crisis [the mysterious family one] is weathered," John tells Dorle on June 3, and his "mental hair has turned snowy white in the last ten days and only the lavish application of alcohol has kept [him] from going mad."

Breaking up by Code

The Dorle I knew seemed even-tempered, but at sixteen she tells her diary "how quickly [her] mood changes." We only have John's trenchant assaults, but Dorle surely volleyed back.

After two months of minimal written communication from John, Dorle receives a typed letter crammed into a smaller envelope informing her that she is "quite right."

"I can only destroy you," John elaborates, "and you can only endanger the security of those I love, yourself included. Your sense of form if nothing else dictates this determination to do something infinitely more important than safety or contentment. Coded or uncoded, I shall bow to your decision and shall not see you unless you ask and perhaps not even then."

Sitting down in the middle of the 2010s at what was once her desk, I attempt some Brooklyn voodoo. With a pen and some notepaper, I try to recapture her coded rejection.

When Quercy, the restaurant at which they dined the most, was out of a particular item, they would cross it out in delicate pencil markings that could be erased whenever it was available again.

I imagine a menu from Quercy arriving at whatever discrete spot Dorle's letters to John were sent. On it, every single item had been delicately crossed off by Dorle. And the following not-really-so-coded message had been written in tiny script in the blank space in between the *aperitifs* and the *plats principaux*.

"From now on, I will dine alone at Quercy at Caravelle at La Gondola. I will not be accompanied by a man who says he loves me but only visits when work requires it, who wants so much more from me than he can possibly deliver."

Then I Google image-search John Carter again.

Those familiar big glasses sit heavy on his

worried face. José Iturbi, Bill Barker, and Georges Asfar were startling handsome, real leading men, but John looks very much the bit player, the Ralph Bellamy, the Bill Pullman. Sometimes, he looks bemused. Other times, stern or annoyed. Not flirtatious, passionate or charismatic. Her friends would be underwhelmed if she were to introduce him, and, fortunately, she was disinclined to broadcast their adulterous affair.

But she feels lost without him. She's got herself anchored to his rollercoasting emotions: distressed when he's distressed, relieved when he's better. Even when she's not with him, she wonders how he's coping. They've gotten so synchronized that even a day passing without word from him makes her uneasy. This self-serious little man has seeped into her skin, and she just can't scrub him off. Her abdomen has turned red and splotchy from her clawing at the eczema that crops up when she's upset. Even her beloved bubble baths don't seem to help.

"This my dear," John concludes [his actual words] "is your receipt, one heart greatly enlarged and badly cracked in exchange for a strange journey, which doesn't exist except for a few seconds in a lifetime," obscure words and far from the end of the street.

Part Two

Rapprochement

The moment Dorle leaves John's life, she wants him back. Endings—like Iturbi's return to Valencia—generally left her sad but relieved. She'd get swept up in the pleasant rhythms of her old life. Except this time nothing feels the same.

One morning soon after the coded rejection, she makes tea and toast with marmalade, quietly slips into her skirt and matching jacket. She walks the lively Midtown streets to Columbia Artists, but the hollowness in her chest makes it hard to breathe. She can't shake her impenetrable melancholy, can't smile at the front desk people with her usual ebullience.

The feeling persists as she arrives at her office, makes the calls to newspapers, answers the queries about concerts, and performs the other duties that make up her routine. She recalls why she'd quit John: his unreliability, his feminine displays of emotions, his poor suffering wife. But an idealized image of him clings determined to her mind, gazing sincerely at her on her couch, toasting her good health like it meant everything in the world to him. Dorle knows she shouldn't, but her pen is in her hand and her note to him soon nearly written.

"You once told me I would never know how much I loved you until I lost you," John tells her on August 14, only three days after his letter accepting her resignation, "you were quite right."

"There is, however, one thing I would like to know, and I want to hear your voice again. Will you telephone me tonight?"

"Darling!" John exclaims when he recognizes Dorle's voice on the phone, like Charles Parnell hearing Kitty O'Shea or Henry VIII's mobile ringing with Anne Boleyn on the line.

"Darling," I hear her echoing, flush with the relief that the off-Broadway drama in which they'd both invested so much emotion isn't closing after all.

A week later, John announces that he is flying to New York just to be with her. He "trembles" at the thought.

Dorle's apartment door rings, she opens it and clutches him in her arms even though he's wet from a summer storm.

Fiber Attack

But just when we assume they are back in gear, Dorle goes to Europe again and receives no correspondence from John between August and late October, when he writes to question the morality of their affair.

"What started out as an attack of strong moral fiber," he exclaims, "turned out to be only a cold in the ear, nose, and throat." Being "neither a European, ironical, nor a Jew," he mistook the symptoms.

He ribs Dorle, an ironical Jew just back from Europe. She is too sophisticated and blasé to be properly concerned with the betrayal of his family.

Dorle sustains the moral fiber, European, and ironical jabs but just doesn't see how she can be too refined to care about his wife.

And what does being Jewish have to do with it?

She's slept with married men before, but never gotten herself so embroiled. She'd thought the problem was John's to deal with since she had no spouse to betray, but then she considers the Jezebels who sleep with married men in the pictures: tasteless, slatternly, not at all how she sees herself.

And John's wife has been out there this whole time, suffering his psychic absence.

Except Dorle is still too caught up in the orbit of John Franklin Carter to let that stop her: the more she sees John, the less she thinks about Sheila.

She and John eat escargot and cassoulet, veal parmigiana, and Chicken Kiev at the Russian Tea Room, accompanied by bottles of claret, brandies and small rounds of martinis once they've made it inside her apartment.

His conversation mirrors his letters—troubles in the agricultural department of the nascent New Deal, the travails of his drunken syphilitic brother. Long fully-formed sentences spill forth from his mouth as Dorle gazes attentively back at this important man who might yet be secretary of state.

After Dark

During those cold winter evenings, after Dorle and John would eat, drink, and talk themselves out, they would shuffle slowly together and make rough enough love to leave scratches on John's back that he complains about in his letters.

I feel drawn to puzzle out the sexual habits of the great-aunt I would undress and put to bed after dinner sixty-odd years later, marveling at the way her long thin breasts drooped down towards her navel. I've never really understood what it meant to be good in bed as sex has always seemed to be more about a connection with a particular person at a particular time, but Dorle in the 1930s suggests otherwise, as her men kept coming back for more.

It's awkward to consider her in the throes of passion: incestuous or just plain icky, like hearing your parents make love, but it's obviously part of the story.

I can speculate better about her sister Faie, another woman from the same background with an epic love life, because I stayed so often with her in New York. At ten or eleven, I remember being regularly confronted by her thin boyish body approaching its eightieth year. She didn't waltz nude around her grandiose rose-colored apartment, but parts of her peeked out often enough from nightgowns, negligees, and towels that I stopped getting embarrassed by it.

She gave me a much more honest education in bodies and sexuality than that Brooke Shields

movie I liked to watch in which she cavorted naked on a desert island with an equally beautiful
male specimen.

Flipping through channels, unable to sleep
one night at Faie's apartment toward the end of
the 1970s, I discovered Channel J, a late-night
Manhattan public-access swinger channel featuring a nude talk show hosted by a bearded, deeply
hairy man, and a camera lingering coarsely on
odd-shaped penises and bushy vaginas. And also
(between station-break advertisements for Pla-
to's Retreat and other swinger's clubs) a show in
which another schlub with a heavy Brooklyn accent roamed the seedier parts of downtown with
his camera, trying to convince women to strip and
pose.

Meanwhile, sleeping nearby in a bedroom
larger than my first Brooklyn apartment, was a
grandmother who refused to let age stymie her
sexuality. She only kicked out her last lover while
in her seventies because he was too messy. ("Dale
is sharing my bed," she had gravely announced
to her son, my father, when Dale first moved in.)
Well into her eighties, she flirted with my friends
when I moved to the city in my early twenties.
One friend created a crude persona based on her,
a nymphomaniac with a high-pitched voice desperate to have sex with anyone or anything from
parking meters to umbrellas. My own first sexual
experiences, which commenced some time in between my pubescent Channel J watching and the
era of my friend's sexist caricature, were pretty
conventional and not nearly as sensual or roman-

tic as I thought they should have been.

Nothing compared to the granddaughters of the nineteenth century Talmudic scholar/banker Sender Jarmulowsky, who escaped their Orthodox Jewish destinies to engage in ecstatic-sounding affairs.

Including Faie's shipboard romance and, in some versions of the story, actual marriage, to Krebs, Hemingway's friend and model for his short story, "Soldier's Home," which lasted only days if not hours after they'd reached dry land.

I found an illustrated volume of poetry, *The Herdboy* by H. Krebs Friend, amidst the boxes of Dorle's letters in my Brooklyn closet, inscribed "to Faie with love from Krebs."

"My body is like a cool hard crystal with fire burning at its core," begins a poem called "Dawn" across from a sentimental figure of a man in an overcoat with a dog in the woods. "Smooth muscles rippling sinuous as snakes awakening, stretching slowly, gracefully out of immobility."

Faie was married at least three times, with lots of lovers in between, and the five sets of letters to her sister Dorle could only be a small fraction of her love life. Which may have disinclined the likes of John Carter from making do with wives with more limited sexual experience.

John's New Job/
The Trouble It Wreaks

Dorle and John's period of frequent meetings

ends abruptly when John takes a new position offered him by FDR.

"If you want me to stay away, of course, I'll stay," John responds to what must have been a savage Dorle letter, "I'll give you warning before I come to New York, so you can depart if you choose."

Of course, John had to take the job. A man determined to be secretary of state couldn't pass up an opportunity to work for the president to hang out with his mistress, but Dorle couldn't stand the thought of it.

"I am bad for you," he goes on, "and you are good for me, and that's the only thing that matters, and life is a conspiracy to prevent things that matter from overcoming things that don't."

They have one of their most querulous quarrels that May.

"Damn you," yells John. "Don't you dare say it was fun. The verb lies in your decision and the adjective is false. Lonely, of course, I'm lonely and so are you, but don't taunt me because we don't cut innocent throats to end loneliness."

The innocent throats belong to his family whom Dorle (seemingly) wants him to abandon.

But even when she broke up with Howard, a boyfriend she had at sixteen, she sounded even-handed, "Love does not seem to fit in the world. I couldn't adjust to the material matter with which I was confronted, and so, in despair, I have given up. I wish, wish, wish I hadn't but perhaps it's better. He is free, so am I."

"Marriage is such a lovely uncertain

affair," she also wrote in her diary at about that time, preternaturally grasping the troubled ones that would come to surround her. "Yes," she concluded, "I would like to undergo that big adventure in life."

Does Dorle really want to go on that adventure with John Franklin Carter? He whined, carried on, broke promises, but clearly hit some powerful nerve. In college, Angela was crushed when someone that she was "not that into" had the gall to leave her, an experience that most of us have had one way or the other. John's slippery ambivalence kept Dorle hooked, his taste for drama infuriating, the intensity of his feelings hard to give up. Did she really want to marry him? I didn't think I'd ever figure that out.

Dear Mother

By the fall of 2016, the mass of papers from Dorle's 55th Street apartment had taken over my Brooklyn closet: her childhood diary; her wedding certificate; a pamphlet signed by Andreotti, oft prime minister of Italy, granting Dario the legion of honor; a collection of old Vatican stamps; and letters, letters, and more letters.

Time had gone by, years spent writing and thinking about Dorle and her lovers, living, as Angela had complained, in Dorle's past rather than my own present. But I had ignored the hundreds of letters to her Orthodox Jewish mother, Grand, as I couldn't imagine Dorle would discuss her love life with her.

On another journey into her papers that spring, though, I finally looked through them and discovered the following: Dorle addressing just that question, whether she really wanted to marry John Carter.

"One of the reasons I would have liked to have married John has very little to do with him personally. I have a terrible need to do something vital in the world before it is too late, and I thought through him and his political knowledge and connections, I could be of some small use. We could have been happy together I think."

Not some burning love or desperate desire to marry and procreate while she still could but a belief in John's importance as a political figure. The letters discuss politics more than music. The situation in Europe subsumed her, destined, as it was, to erupt again in a few short years.

And New York as well. Period photographs show beggars, breadlines, protests, and desperate salesmen, trying to hawk everything they possibly can, though there wasn't much trace of any of that between Columbia Artists and Dorle's apartment in her neighborhood of glamorous dresses in department store windows. Despite the bank failure a couple of decades before, Dorle had landed on the comfortable side of the daunting chasm between rich and poor, but the painful condition of the rest of the city, the country, preyed on her. Remaining loyal to a serious New Dealer could have assuaged her guilt just a little. She may not have had fruit, or bread, or pennies for every starving sufferer, but her lover was working with her president to fix their troubles.

The Telegram

Back in 1934, a couple of years before Dorle's letter to her mother, John grows increasingly nervous about losing Dorle for good. The next time she calls things off, she might stick to her guns.

On May 16, he calls her and asks "point blank" whether she wants to see him again, only to realize, humiliatingly enough, that Dorle's mother rather than Dorle had picked up the phone.

For the next several days, John besieges Dorle with letters (several each day) demanding to know their status.

When finally, on May 18th, he receives a reassuring telegram from her, he declares that "If I hadn't found your telegram waiting, I would have left here to find you, ending home, job, reputation in one shot," a gesture worthy of Dorle's *Master Lovers* if only he'd acted on it.

Dorle, at her desk, comes across those lines and groans out loud at his claim to have been about to abandon everything for her if only she had ignored his desperate letters. Or maybe she chuckled instead, already skeptical of John's hyperbole.

In fact, after celebrating the reception of her telegram, John already starts to pull back.

"I have never wanted anything more than to

be with you … but my time is now sewed up in committee meetings and all kinds of New Dealership. Darling, I love you."

Neither Dante, Byron, Henry the Eighth or any other Master Lover was ever "sewed up" in a committee meeting. John wants Dorle to be on hold, available for the occasional sexcapade, but to understand the sacrosanctity of his work and family.

Meanwhile, he remains enraptured by coded communication.

"If you send me a telegram, sign it Watson as they have an embarrassing habit of making me initial copies of telegrams which arrive unsigned."

"I loathe all this business of deceit," concludes FDR's future spy.

By the age of sixteen, Dorle was already tiring of boys: from Howard ("he is free, and now am I") to the young George Cukor, whom she was "too temperamental to see … steadily." By the point John is demanding that she call herself Watson in telegrams, they have already been together for several years.. Years of melodrama, of guilt, of excruciating changes of heart. Her feelings had to be flagging. At least a little?

What if subways could be time machines? I could take the G to the A to the F to her 57th Street apartment in the middle of the 1930s, having magically grown period clothing so as not to alarm her with my slumpy twenty-first century attire.

"Do you still love him?" I insist.

"Do you still feel the same?"

I call up photos of her from about that time, look into her eyes and wait for an answer that might not really be an answer at all, just a wan, wry smile, beginning to see the irony in the situation, even the humor.

But not yet ready to extricate herself and move on.

Love and Anger

They make a date to see each other in July, and in John's letters leading up to that date, he ecstatically counts the days until the meeting is set to occur, but his letters slip silently past it as if there had never been a plan.

In August he declares "that I love you and that I love you and that I love you." And questions his marriage for the first time, declaring that he "seriously" doubts the "desirability of the whole show," an off-hand remark that may have meant something to Dorle.

And makes me ponder poor Sheila out shopping in Washington as she does on bad days, sensing in John's cold and distant behavior an ineffable threat to her security.

Not surprisingly, when they finally see each other in August, something goes terribly wrong.

I imagine them returning to Quercy, attempting to ride the clock back to more comfortable times. After they have made love and are lying shoulder to shoulder in Dorle's plush, king-sized bed, Dorle asks John why he'd called his marriage an "undesirable show."

But John, all too talented at switching back and forth between different versions of reality, shoots her a look and pontifically lays out his obligation to this family, a holy bond that no silly woman can be permitted to tear asunder.

Dorle's heart slams back and forth inside her chest and she pants for breath like she's been punched in the stomach. He'd been the one to cast doubt on his marriage. All she'd done was ask for clarification. She'd thought she'd been okay, able to take John with a grain of salt. But he'd stuck his grubby little fingers inside her psyche again, making her gnash her teeth in frustration.

"I very much doubt if I can live more days like Friday," he writes her afterwards. "You in your arrogance conceive that I am incapable of suffering, but I feel ghastly and shaken to the roots."

After that terrible Friday in 1934, a year of epistolary silence fell between John and Dorle, not a single letter from August of 1934 to August of 1935, at least not one that Dorle chose to save.

Booze Cruise

John's next missive, a series of letters stuffed into the same envelope, picks up casually as if they'd been in mid-conversation.

A year later finds him on a cut-rate booze cruise to Bermuda. In terrible, drunken, middle-class company, John yearns for Dorle, a beacon of elegance and restraint when she doesn't want to kill him.

"*Liebe Dorlinke*," he addresses her, then, without further ado, relates the sorry tale of life aboard ship.

"My roommate is an extroverted, genial 'call me Bill' drunk. I am staying in the cabin and adjusting to the type.

"I had more sandwiches and three highballs with him [the roommate] and he immediately conveyed to me his intention to bring more women into the cabin. I said that I did not object but could not participate."

"Dinner was terrible," he goes on, "a drunken dentist named Warren, a drunken Brooklyn businessman named Bernard, a friend of Dick Simon named Vettleman, my drunken roommate and myself."

"*Ach Gott*," John (surely drunk by now too) interrupts himself, "why aren't you with me on a clean ship heading for somewhere not marred with vulgarity and mail order catalogue *bonhomie*?"

"Darling, I love you," John goes on. "I've told you before, but you don't believe me. But I do. I am obeying the law of the jungle and going back to my den."

The law of the jungle orders us to stay in our den with our wives, but John has only reluctantly returned to his and can't get Dorle off his mind.

What really bothers him about the "healthy spring animals" on board are the gender dynamics of their pick-up scene.

"Unfortunately, the scales had fallen off my eyes, and I saw people as they really were—women with dreadful half-starved looks prowling around, flaunting their charms, and men with silly fatuous conceit, taking their irresistibility for granted. Once on the deck, I saw a little man walking alone with two hungry women in pursuit. Their paths crossed and I averted my eyes. It was too much like the pounce of a cat or a spider."

James Thurber's *New Yorker* cartoons of that era come to mind, enormous blob-shaped females chasing after testicularly challenged little men. I don't know where John gets his oddly misogynist vision of "pinch-mouthed women" hunting "sad-eyed men," but he looks the part: meek, bespectacled, fragile. The real point of his depiction of these cruise-ship sharpies, however, is to establish the ideal alternative, a female too elegant and demure to engage in the chase.

"Earlier in the evening," John goes on, "I found a pleasant woman named Nan Feldman with whom I declared a truce at once, so we talked, danced and drank with that completely mutual ease which only lovers or total strangers can achieve. Probably I liked her because she faintly suggested you—dark, slight, Jewish, with a keen mind and a quick intuition.

"However, the night wore on. She retired. I went to bed, but before I could sleep my roommate appeared with a honeymoon couple and the chief steward and sat talking until all hours. I got bored and went to sleep. It struck me as a hell of a way to spend one's honeymoon, anyway. I didn't admit to myself that I didn't try to shift my cabin because I couldn't bear to be alone."

This twisted version of Madonna/whore with smart Jewish Madonnas and avaricious cruise sluts is really a desperate cry for Dorle, and John ends the collection of boozy letters that he had stuck into the same envelope by informing her that "when I come back to New York, I shall contrive to telephone you just to make sure you are in this world for that is very important to me. Goodbye darling, and good luck until we meet again, which will not be long deferred except by your choice. Perhaps in the autumn we shall be together a little."

John hasn't seen Dorle for months, and his image of her has morphed: not the wild animal Jewess that needed to be beaten or the infuriated shrew whipping off angry letters and demanding that he show up in New York, but a genteel, demure woman contrasting with the crass creatures surrounding him. For both John Carter and Bill Barker, and [her other lovers as we will see, Dorle filled metaphoric voids, her New York Jewishness, her sexually confident otherness mutable qualities that meant something different for each man.

Love as a Cure for Love

Their relationship seems tenuous at best, but that December, when Dorle sails to Europe again, she feels obligated to tell him that she can't promise to be faithful.

Unusual ethics, needing to tell the married man with whom you'd occasionally been sleeping that you may choose to sleep with someone else. And if Dorle's so intent on transparency, what does she think about Sheila, John's wife, going about her days for years now with no idea about what has been happening?

"It would please you to know," John responds, "that the thought of your experimenting with love as a cure for love does not disturb me. You cannot give anyone what I have, so you cannot destroy anything, only hurt the silly part of me that is savage where you are concerned."

More Mixed Messages

Tanned from boats and deserts and a little bit plump from exotic meals on a trip (about which we know from the men who cured her love with love), Dorle returns home to find a barrage of confusing messages from John Franklin Carter. She opens the letters in the morning while sipping strong tea with milk and sugar in her living room. The sun shines through the window onto her face, and she feels strangely disengaged from the dramas inside the white envelopes.

There is no indication of when they may see each other again.

"My absence is not entirely due to force majeure," he tells her coyly, "though force majeure has determined it so far."

That December morning, Dorle recalls how devastated she would have been just a year or so before by the thought of John staying away on purpose. Briefly, she pangs for the grand folly that had once been her love for him, but falling in and out of love is old hat for her. In her teen diary, nearly twenty years before, she explains her feeling for a poor young man. "The inevitable has happened ... I no longer feel the same."

On another morning not long afterwards, Dorle allows John's sudden announcement that she is "meant to love and bear my children" to pierce her thickening skin. Her big brown eyes well with tears as she does want children but is growing too old. She loves her sister's four-year-old, Tony, my father, but it's not the same as having her own. She once fantasized about having many, many of them. "You and your thirteen children, I and my secretary of state," John once said of their different life goals. John's career with the agricultural department of the New Deal isn't exactly growing by leaps and bounds, and the possibility of children slips further away from Dorle each year.

Later in that same letter, John tells her that she "must not be cheated of life because I have the queer determination to keep my word [to

Sheila] as long as humanly possible." Dorle reads his words, takes a deep breath and notes to herself the frantic questions his words might once have raised. Why did he call his determination "queer"? How long was "as humanly possible"?

Lady Macbeth

In early 1935, John begins to talk about his wife for the first time. The tempered, gentle, sad-sounding woman whose diary I'd read, jokes John, was actually a descendant of Lady Macbeth.

In August of that year, nearly three years after they met on the *Île de France*, John tells Dorle how he and his wife got together.

"Shortly after the war, I met my wife in Paris and fell in love with her on the spot. That too [like him and Dorle] was nothing which could easily arrange itself. She had a badly injured husband and two small kids, so instead of being gay and careless I undertook to save the whole family. I did. I got her husband to take a job, which was waiting for me in America, and took the responsibility of pulling the entire family through. The operation was successful and eventually she fell in love with me, there was a divorce, and we married."

John's message was clear. He could not leave his wife as she'd left her husband for him.

In January of 1937, towards the end of their long correspondence, John informs Dorle that his wife's mental illness has landed her in an institution, and that their affair is at least partially to blame.

"I have had long consultations with psychiatrists and as far as it seems pertinent to the problem I give the most complete picture…They know I am in love with another woman, and nothing can be done about it."

Could the affair have really driven Sheila crazy? What really happened between Dorle, Sheila, and John would remain a mystery until I discovered another letter Dorle wrote to her mother from about that time.

"Mother dear. It's hard to write. The past few weeks have not been easy. As perhaps you have guessed I had rather hoped to straighten out the pattern of my life this winter. For a number of years, as you know, John and I have been deeply attached to each other … I was tremendously interested in his work and he has been to New York so much more than ever before that the situation in its present form became impossible. Though it is always painful for me to make decisions to force issues, I finally insisted that John tell his wife the complete truth in every detail, an issue he had never faced before because of her ill health. The upshot was that she came to New York and I met her. She was, as I knew she would be, a fine good woman. We talked at length—I feeling more and more detached as I went along. The end was inevitable. She was right. I was right. John was right, and there was no solution but to consider the happiness of the greatest number of people. And so John went back to Washington and I haven't written or spoken to him since."

The two women did not convene at Dorle's apartment, where she had made love so often with John, but someplace quiet and solitary: a department store restaurant at an off hour, a hotel bar. Sheila and Dorle sit across from each other sipping sherry or sweet vermouth, softly listening and talking, tears in both of their eyes.

Back in 1932, a couple of months after finding Dorle's destroyed letter to her husband, Sheila became obsessed with a play by the Irish playwright Thomas Moore and concluded her diary with a song he wrote. She called it her epitaph.

> *Does time with its cold wing whither*
> *Each feeling that once was dear?*
> *Then child of misfortunate come hither.*
> *I'll weep with thee, tear for tear.*

Last Night

"Am I becoming a materialist?" Dorle asked herself in 1917. "Have dates and engagements filled my life to such an extent that ideas and ambitions pale by contrast and gradually fade away. No, I answer, emphatically no." Again and again, Dorle berates herself in her diary for what she felt to be her fatuous and flirtatious nature, not caring sufficiently about the people who were suffering and risking their lives like the American soldiers just then heading for Europe.

A decade and a half later, she may have seen

her relationship with John as a way to have it all. She got to have love and romance with a man doing something "vital" in the world.

Did John and Dorle really cut things off after her meeting with Sheila? Let's give them one last night.

John arrives around midnight at her apartment after both of their separate social obligations have been fulfilled.

He rings the melodious bell, and she comes to the door to usher him in.

Coolly and calmly, after a drink or two of whisky, they stroll from the living room into her bedroom. They fuck quietly and efficiently without fanfare.

John does not spend the night and share Dorle's regular breakfast: crisp toast, marmalade, strong milky tea.

Not long after slipping out of Dorle, John would have slipped out of her apartment and her life. She would have turned over, sighed, and fallen asleep as he drunkenly, desultorily slunk back to his hotel, poignantly aware that if this was not the last time, the last time was surely nigh.

Viereck!

Okay, their last night, but how did the affair *really* end?

Dorle's letter to her mother suggested that Dorle ended it herself out of concern for Sheila, but an undated letter from John, living outside of its envelope in the back of one of Dorle's dresser drawers, implies that John plugged the plug.

"I shall probably never see you again. This is neither reaction nor repentance—it is simply the realization that to see each other would be fatal for us both. You have made me very happy and very unhappy. I am sure to repent of this action, but I shall not take it back."

We don't know if John changed his mind, if that really was the end. A series of undated letters suggest that political differences had also gotten wedged between them: the question of Germany, Austria, and the Jews. As well as John's reference in another undated letter to a questionable German named George Viereck, who would become infamous in just a few more years.

It was okay, John reassured Dorle, to contribute to the defense funds of the Scottsboro Boys and Sacco and Vanzetti, but if she followed the lead of Mayor Fiorello La Guardia, an Italian Jew, and ceased to support Bruno Hauptman, the German man accused of kidnapping the Lindberg baby, there would be "an explosion of Anti-Jewish feeling that will be bitter and bigoted beyond anything that has been seen in this country." David Wilentz, the man prosecuting Hauptman, was a Jew, and despite Lindbergh's well-known anti-semitism, a conspiracy theory at the time had the Jews persecuting Hauptmann.

"Don't be annoyed with me for writing this," John concludes. "Today I'm in a mood of frustration and despair, and I wish I were with you."

In another letter, John urges her to be "cautious" about boycotting Germany and Austria for their anti-Jewish actions, as that would be akin to "the Hitler whim of rejecting a culture for purely racial reasons."

Equating boycotting Germany and Austria over their treatment of the Jews with Hitler's own anti-Semitism makes me think of the "White Lives Matter," slogan, the bizarre implication that white people weren't being properly appreciated after the murder of George Floyd.

Next, John hits Dorle where it hurts suggesting that if these boycotts occurred, then "Maestro [her beloved Toscanini] might not be allowed to perform Brahms [who was Austrian] in Vienna." Dorle should not boycott, according to John, "what is beautiful or attractive or simply useful because you disapprove of the politics of those who produce it."

I don't like to think these arguments had an impact on Dorle, but she once responded to my father's query about her friend, Elizabeth Schwarzkopf's close relationship with Goebbels by declaring that "great art should be separated from politics."

The idea of boycotting Germany and Austria was unpopular with most Americans. It may not necessarily have been the only strategy. But in another letter from about the same time, John goes beyond his opposition to boycotting Nazis to reveal that he may be a suspected Nazi himself.

"George Viereck was in town yesterday and informed me that my name was in the files of the

Dickstein committee as a Nazi agent. He said he got this from a close friend of his in New York who had seen the Dickstein documents."

After I'd learned about the Jarmulowsky bank default towards the end of Dorle's life, I managed to question her about it, however painful and embarrassing it may have been, but if I'd stumbled upon this letter from John while she'd been alive, I don't think I would have had the courage to ask her if her married lover had been a Nazi agent.

She is no longer alive to ask. And the McCormack-Dickstein congressional report about German agents in America does not, in fact, list Carter.

But George Viereck was most certainly a Nazi, an important one. Rachel Maddow, in her fall 2022 podcast *Ultra*, refers to him as "the top banana" of Nazi infiltrators in late thirties to early forties America.

Viereck transmitted propaganda direct from Nazi Germany to millions of Americans.

Senator Ernest Lundeen of Minnesota (who died in a mysterious plane crash. Listen to the podcast for the whole lurid story) published pro-German editorials in major newspapers that were actually penned by Viereck. After Lundeen's death, it was revealed that he and countless other senators and congresspeople were deluging their constituents with Viereck's Nazi propaganda, using their "franking" privileges, by which members of Congress can send mail for free.

John talks of Viereck like Dorle knows him, but he seldom introduced people in his letters.

"As though my interest in modern Germany," John concludes his Viereck discussion, "proved I was in Hitler's pay or against the Jews. The anti-Hitler organization has a pleasant trick of writing editors and publishers anonymously and confidentially warning them that so and so is a paid propagandist ... Also in these cases, private detectives have been put on the trail of those suspected of harboring anti-Jewish sentiments."

Dorle, a Jew, is asked to sympathize with those targeted for their anti-Jewish activities and to accept that Carter was simply studying modern Germany out of intellectual curiosity.

We don't know how much the Viereck reference and these tangles with John over Germany, Austria, and Jews impacted their relationship, but by the time the news of *Kristallnacht* hit America not long afterwards, their correspondence had ceased. Dorle, a religious reader of the morning *New York Times*, would have seen the headline on November 11, 1938—*Nazis Smash, Loot and Burn Jewish Shops and Temples Until Goebbels Calls Halt: Jews are beaten*—and the subheading *Furniture and goods are flung from homes and shops. 1500 are Jailed, 20 now are suicides* and been relieved, at least I think so, to no longer be sleeping (or associating) with a German apologist.

And by the early 1940s, Carter's old friend, Viereck, was becoming a household name.

Dorle had a distinct morning ritual.

After concluding her ablutions and walking across the apartment to the kitchen, she would brew herself a pot of black tea. She would toast bread (or panettone during the holidays) and spread butter and marmalade upon it.

After opening the *New York Times* across the expansive dining room table, she would pore over it.

Starting in the fall of 1939, more and more stories about Viereck began to appear.

October 1939: *Eight more register as foreign agents: G.S. Viereck is one of those with German principals.*

March, 1940: *City club disturbed by Heckler's shouts. Man interrupts Viereck to call him a Nazi Agent.*

Christmas Eve, 1940, wasn't safe from reading about Viereck in the morning paper. *Viereck, Nazi agent, quit overseas club. Resignation had been requested by foreign correspondents.*

Did Dorle worry that morning, while pouring more milk into her tea, crunching that last piece of toast, and wiping the sides of her mouth with her napkin that Carter himself had been an agent? Viereck said that he'd been listed in the Dickstein Report.

Years before, John had praised a book that Viereck had once written, something about the wandering Jew. He'd spoken frequently to Dorle of his great love for the Jews, the sensuality of their women. One evening in 1933, he'd insisted they retire to the bedroom though they had not yet gone out for dinner. Bruch's Hebrew epic, *Kol Nidre,* was being performed on the radio, and it would make a stunning background for their lovemaking.

She had been sensible enough to refuse. It was a dreary piece anyway, and she was in no mood for sudden sex. She'd grown more and more confused over the years, though, about how John could have such rapt admiration for her people while seeming so untroubled by events in Germany and Austria. Perhaps making love with a Jewess was excitingly louche. Mother was cross enough with Dorle for ceasing to go to temple. What would she think of the man she been inviting into her bed?

Carter did work for Roosevelt, though, and Dorle's old pal George Biddle, whose brother, Francis, was attorney general had seemed to vouch for Carter when Dorle had brought him up years before.

But Viereck. Viereck!

Each time she sees his name, her shoulders shudder as if she's suddenly cold.

And she imagines John responding to the news, his cheekbones scrunched together in that oddly rat-like way, defending his friend as if all the accusations were absurd.

"Gestapo," she can just hear John's incredulous tone, "Not every German ..."

After their marriage in 1942, Dario joined her in the morning at the breakfast table. Not as avid a reader as she was, he used the *Times* to work on his English.

Dorle had not exactly told or not told Dario about her lovers. It was his male prerogative not to tell her of his. In the stories that she *did* tell him, the line between friendship, flirtation, and affair had been carefully muddied. Briefly, she'd mentioned Georges and Bill while staying clear of Albert, J.B.S. and certainly John as they had all been married at the time. It was enough of a stretch to ask Dario, twelve years younger, to remain faithful, impossible if he were to learn how little concern she had for injured wives.

Over the years of their courtship, more news came in from Europe, the Nazis taking country after country, endangering Jews as they went. Grajewo, where Dorle's grandfather had been born, had fallen with the rest of Poland. She and Dario acknowledged these events without particularly discussing them, as, what, after all, was there to say. Of Dario's parents in Italy, Uncle Arturo, Zia Lidia and the rest, they barely spoke at all. Dario preferred to shoulder his fears on his own.

But when, on the morning of March 26, 1942, she reads that Viereck had been convicted of false registry, "axis propaganda in speeches signed by Viereck," she gasps audibly. Pro-German speeches made on the floor of congress, editorials in countless newspapers, millions of fliers sent over the mail written by that friend of John Carter's.

An attack of indigestion, she tells Dario,

wishing immediately that she'd found a less indelicate excuse.

Alone in the bathroom, she sits on the toilet, pondering what she'd read, flushing after a few minutes to maintain the ruse.

Washing and drying her hands, she walks back to Dario, pleased to see him buried in the paper himself, not particularly concerned about her sudden distress.

Dorle walks restlessly over to the window and watches the men in suits and hats drift by.

Her mind heaves, twisted by everything inside it.

However much she may once have wanted a more permanent connection with John, she is certainly relieved that he is gone from her life.

Ironic, she thinks, as her eyes drift back to the newspaper, the headline about Viereck; Carter had always sought greater notoriety but not of that nature.

Wherever he is, with Sheila in Washington, off on some agricultural department errand for the president, he's surely heard the news.

Though whoever he is meeting with might have no idea that he's been associated with a Nazi propagandist.

But then again, people know remarkably little about each other. The families of Goldsmith, their tailor on Broadway, Mrs. Eisenstein, who cleans up after their parties, Jacop, the egg man, may have lost their money at the bank on Canal Street. Twenty-odd years earlier, the Jarmulowskys had been in the morning paper nearly as frequently as Viereck, none of it good. As she had become Jarmel, then Soria, the Jews who worked for them may not have made the connection.

But if Dorle and Dario's clothes or parties or meals were suddenly sabotaged, she knows who to suspect. A Jew who'd lost his money had nearly stabbed Meyer to death. That was decades ago, but anger doesn't just evaporate.

Postscript: Percy

My paternal grandfather lurks over the story of Dorle and John.

According to family lore, Percy committed one, possibly two, crimes against Dorle. He abandoned her sister, Faie, when she was pregnant with my father.

The second crime is harder to figure. Percy had headed up the southern-European and northern-African divisions of the Office of War Information, a precursor to the CIA, before being fired by Eisenhower, ostensibly for leaking news of US prison camps holding German and Italian soldiers. While at the State Department, according to the family story, Percy had refused to use his State Department connections to help Dario get American citizenship and may have intentionally attempted to scuttle the deal.

But the accusation came into question after I found Dorle and Dario's wedding announcement in the *Times* entitled "Dorle Jarmel, A Bride" and learned that Dario was working at the Office of

War Information at the time of their wedding. It seemed likely that Percy had gotten him the job.

True or false, the terrible story of what Percy did to Dario made me assume Dorle had cut him off cold in the 1940s. But John Carter wrote the following to her in 1959: "The enemies of my youth are dearer to me than my friends of yesterday—since that is my definition of old age. I still have a bit to go and you—as Percy says—are holding up wonderfully."

Not only did John and Percy know each other, almost an inevitability as we will see, but Percy, despite his crimes, conveyed updates between Dorle and her long-ago lover.

Percy and John

Percy was in Italy covering Mussolini in the early 1920s, writing for the *New York Evening Post* and the *United Press*. Chummy with Mussolini after traveling with him and the press corps in North Africa, Percy was allowed to write both the questions and the answers (both of which easily passed the Fascist censors) for what became the first American interview of Il Duce.

And John was there at the same time, the *New York Times*' correspondent. American journalists in Rome all knew each other.

Percy had fascist sympathies at the time, and John may have, too, if his apparent approval of Goering a decade later was any indication.

Both men enjoyed grand political assertions.

They dine alfresco in the Piazza Navona late on a steaming mid-summer evening a decade or so before the *Île de France*. The water bounces off the gods in the Bernini fountains, cigarette smoke and leisurely Italian conversation fill the air, and two young Americans drink white wine and make fascist pronouncements, unaware of their future synchronicity.

John has no idea that the dour American in the white suit and patrician accent (who is really a Jewish, working-class-Brooklyn boy') will marry the sister of a woman who will dominate his life.

And Percy is unaware that the *Times* reporter with the big glasses and uncomfortable-looking suit will have an agonizing affair with the sister of his future wife.

CHAPTER 6
FRIDAYS IN THE NINETIES

By the early 1990s, Dorle's regular, not very master-lover-like Friday evening visitor was me, as I had landed back in New York after a stint in graduate school in Arizona. She took me out to the old-fashioned French and Italian restaurants still open on 55th Street.

Quite deaf, increasingly blind, and clinging vigorously to a cane (which she called her stick), she would smoke her cigarettes, drink her gin, and answer candidly whatever question I threw at her, however personal. She revealed a female flirtation from her youth, shared openly the fact that her interest in sex outlasted Dario's, and would have told me anything I wanted to know. I was not yet aware of the bank failure and would not learn about her 1930s love affairs for nearly twenty more years, so, star-struck by her glittery past, I mostly just listed famous people and asked if she'd met them.

"Frank Sinatra?"

"No."

"Eleanor Roosevelt."

"Yes."

Sometimes I requested favorite stories such as how she'd accompanied George Bernard Shaw to a concert at Royal Albert Hall only to be mortified when he'd refused to stand for "God Save the King."

But Dorle's once labyrinthian social world had been shrinking. By the mid-1990s, only myself, Angela, and Tobias and Floriano, two elderly gay men whom Dorle referred to as "the boys," still visited her regularly, while she lost much of her sight and her mind grew muddled.

My evenings with her grew more and more precious as time went by. Even now, decades on, the details of our Friday evening rituals keep coming back to me. The struggle to get her old restaurant matchbooks to light, the warm acrid smell of cigarette smoke, the solidity of Dorle's presence on the faded couch across from the armchair. At dinner, the Colombian waiter at the Italian restaurant across the street, who used the word "fantastico" so frequently that it became Angela's and my private nickname for him, would smile beneficently down upon us as we ordered veal chops, carbonaras, panna cottas and glasses of wine.

One evening, I had been forced to sneak in through the unlocked trash alcove when Dorle didn't answer the door and found her dressed for dinner but fast asleep.

Her eyes opened when I called her name, and she asked politely like an obedient little girl if she could please be allowed five more minutes.

When she finally awoke and I suggested returning another day, her face blistered with disappointment.

We went to La Bonne Soupe, the restaurant a couple of doors down from her building where she often dined alone—propped up at the bar where smoking was still allowed by a kind French waiter—and walked home by a sad-faced Norman maître d', who had been mysteriously absent for the last two weeks.

In the middle of a sentence a few minutes into our meal, Dorle suddenly flinched and looked quizzically around her.

I asked her how she felt, but she just looked blankly back at me.

"And how are the children, Winston?" she finally pulled herself together to ask. I had no children and knew no Winston.

"Tony," she called me next, my father's name, looking pleased with herself for getting it right, "I'm sorry I'm not better company tonight."

Then she closed her eyes, leaned back on her chair and fell briefly asleep.

A few minutes later, she opened them again and slowly began to recover from what may have been a mini stroke.

On our way back to the apartment, she smiled for the first time that evening, pride lighting up her cheeks, the memory of a latter-day Master Lover.

Later, I learned that the Norman Maître D had moved on to a pricier restaurant, but Dorle insisted that the hopelessly smitten man had been fired for walking her home.

As Dorle aged, she would lean more and more heavily on me as we slowly made our way back from Fantastico's. Once in her bedroom, I would help her remove her dress, her jewels, her enormous bras.

I would stand outside her bathroom as she peed and brushed her teeth, then help her into bed and kiss her goodnight on the cheek. The leap from walking her to her apartment and bidding her goodbye at the door to helping her undress and tucking her in had happened spontaneously without comment from either of us, and I like to think it involved an evolving intimacy, not just the intensifying of her needs.

During our dinners and our cocktail hours, we'd sometimes fall into silence. Dorle's pupils would dance around her eyes, and her mind would journey long ago and far away.

Maybe to Lisbon, during Master Lover days, where Manuel the Second "at the age of nineteen … mounted the throne of Portugal rotten with age and corruption." Or to Tahiti where creepy Paul Gauguin met Tehura "bathing in a blue stream against a background of lime and mango trees … only thirteen, but a woman by Tahitian standards … shy and beautiful in a primitive, perfect way."

Or maybe to a comforting desert meal with Georges Asfar in Syria. "We were covered with dust, but ten minutes later the two men had served us a table with tea, toast, honey, apricot jam and eggs, beautiful silver dishes—most extraordinary."

CHAPTER SEVEN
THE ORIENTAL MASTER

"The European, whose sensibility tours the Orient, is a watcher, never involved, always detached, always ready for new examples of what the Description de l'Egypte called 'bizarre jouissance.' The Orient becomes a living tableau of queerness." — Edward Said

I had struggled to read the handwriting of the letters from Georges Asfar, the man that I'd been hearing about since childhood, but it got much easier when Sheila Canby and Mecka Baumeister of the Metropolitan Museum borrowed them in search of insight into his Ottoman room and gave their interns the frustrating job of transcribing them.

I sorted through them until I found the earliest one, April 24, 1935, a letter that should tell me exactly how they met.

But what became immediately clear as I struggled through Georges's elliptical grammar and frequent French words was that they already knew each other well. It was written in the midst of their affair. Seventy years had passed since then. There was no way to know where they actually met. But, surely, Dorle would have chosen to meet Georges, her Oriental lover, not in the dirty Depression-era streets of the city in which she had been born, but instead among the souks and minarets of his native Syria.

Damascus 1932

Wide-eyed child Dorle, *Arabian Nights* in hand, had summoned handsome sultans in flowing garb, whispery genies granting wishes. She'd conjured the silken voice of Scheherazade herself, telling a thousand and one tales of a magical, mystical world that would make any normal, turn-of-the-last-century poor little rich New York Jewish girl yearn for distant desert kingdoms.

Once child Dorle had grown to adult Dorle and had begun sailing back and forth across the Atlantic, it was only a matter of time before she made her way to the Middle East.

Long before Dario, several decades before my own birth, I think she visited Damascus.

In 1932, it is in French hands, a tense respite between struggles for independence.

Donkeys and carts clog the streets and only the occasional automobile rumbles by. The craggy medina artisans look like they're from the Middle Ages.

Dorle has gone on one of her tours of Europe, then taken off to the Middle East. Later she would take the Lloyd Triestino Line and meet Bill Barker, but now she rides the Orient Express to Istanbul and a less iconic train to Damascus.

She stays at the recently built art deco Grand Orient Hotel in Hijaz Square, its resplendent white stones glimmering over the skyline.

On her first day, tired from the long journey and disoriented by the heat, she remains at the hotel, cooled by ceiling fans and cocktails, and dines alone at its Ali Baba restaurant.

The following morning, wearing a blue dress with white polka dots that she worries is too cutesy, she proceeds to the medina in the heart of the old city. The percussive hawking of wares reminds her of the discordant music considered shocking in her childhood: *The Rite of Spring, Pierrot lunaire.*

Later, Dorle will describe the medina to her mother.

"All of the business is done in bazaars or '*souks*' and each souk is dedicated to a specialty —cloth or saddles and decorations for donkeys and horses, cord, wool, leather slippers, '*keffiehs*' which are the flowing clothes the Arabs wear on their head, trunks, kitchen things."

Only occasionally does she glimpse westerners, probably French, in European dress, but no one particularly notes her atypical attire and lighter, though already sun-burned, skin.

As she has been charged by Arthur Judson, the man who runs the Stadium Concerts back in New York to buy a "fine" but "affordable" Oriental carpet, she stops a grizzly, smoking Frenchman and asks where the best carpets are to be had. "*Tapis de qualités,*" she calls them, noting the sweat stains on the man's white shirt, the dirt under his fingernails, and worrying that he was too proletarian to have much idea about quality.

But he resonantly responds, "Souk Hamidiyah," delicately touches her shoulder blade, allowing her a whiff of strong cologne, and points her in the right direction.

"*Le meillure d'Hamidiyah?*" she asks, the best place in the Souk Hamidiyah. "Asfar," the Frenchman exclaims without a moment's hesitation. It's the first time she hears the name. "*Ç'est d'Asfar.*" With a wry wave, the Frenchmen is off, leaving her alone in the teeming market.

"The shop of the Asfars is the most important bazaar in the Souk Hamdie," she will later boast to her mother.

Taking a deep breath and steeling her courage, she takes off in the direction suggested by the Frenchmen. Quickly, she slips forward past knife salesmen, perfume venders, goats, and goat hides.

At the next white face she sees, she points in the direction in which she heads for confirmation, "Hamdie?"

"*Oui, ç'est ca.*"

Not many steps farther, she sees an ornate stone arch with the words "Souk Hamdie" imprinted upon it.

At that very moment, better quality Arabs—some in western dress, some in robes—approach, grabbing her hands and pulling her toward their stores.

"Asfar," she declares.

"Asfar," she repeats like a spell.

The discouraged salesmen mutter disparagingly.

"*Mais où est le magasin Asfar?*" she demands.

And unexpectedly, a teenage boy with long

beautiful eyelashes beats his way through the touts.

"*Magasin Asfar, Madame,*" he tells Dorle, "*viens avec moi.*"

"The Asfar shop is the largest in the city," Dorle will later describe it, "jammed haphazardly with Roman antiques, old swords, rugs, brocades, seventeenth-century robes, old faiences, Hittite remains."

The lovely boy disappears the moment they enter the dusty Asfar domain, leaving Dorle crouched hesitantly between a huge vase that looks Chinese and a broken Roman torso of a woman with a luxuriant stomach and one medium-sized breast.

The next person to enter, a handsome man in his early thirties with dark hair and more southern European than Arabic features, wears the requisite white suit, favored by westerners in the tropics. Grabbing her hand, he performs a low, nearly Japanese bow, and apologizes for having kept her waiting.

"Englishmen," he whispers, looking askance, had been taking up his time but now he is all hers.

She tries to explain as best she can, apologizing for troubling him and trying to describe the sort of carpet required by Judson.

Grabbing her hand once more, Georges Asfar frowns slightly to indicate that there are niceties they must perform before business can be transacted. In his odd French/Arabic accent, he explains that he has carpets of all types and prices, but surely they must drink coffee first.

Snapping his fingers at the boy, who turns out to have already reentered the room, he commands that it be brought for them.

"Arab coffee," Dorle would later write, "is very strong, bitter, flavored with something which looks like an almond, but I think is a cardamom seed."

The next room of the store, into which they stride a moment later, delicate demitasses in their hands, is filled with intricately shaped, bold-colored ceramics, the one after that transported without alteration from the glory days of the Ottoman era: chairs, divans, wooden carvings with abstract designs.

When Dorle sighs, shakes her head and confesses that his carpets may be more than she can pay, a perfectly constructed panic passes through Georges's face, quickly replaced by a winning smile.

"*Si le mademoiselle* [a bold assumption] *n'as pas l'argent pour acheter un tapis, elle a besoin de manger avec moi*. I know the perfect place."

And there is little reason to refuse. She has romantic entanglements in New York, but in the Orient one leaves one's past behind. Being taken out to dinner will not be bad, as the extravagance of the journey has stretched her finances. And while under normal circumstances, she might hesitate to dine with a shopkeeper, she must consider the elegance of the shop and of the person. He's handsome too, even if his nose is a tad too Semitic like her own.

And the restaurant where Georges takes her that evening after picking her up at her hotel takes her breath away, an enormous dining room in an old Ottoman house in an affluent neighborhood overlooking the city. The ceramic tiles on the floor and table explode in colorful squares, cubes, and circles.

Many of the diners, unlike the meager tourists at Dorle's hotel restaurant, have robes, fezzes and other forms of Oriental dress. The western men wear perfect summer suits like out of the cinema, and the women tend towards scanty dresses in the twenties mode though the thirties had already begun, the market back home having recently crashed.

The meze is pungently spiced and generously portioned. The delicately grilled fish that follows somehow fits into their stomachs along with the honeyed desserts, the sharp coffee, the wine and the digestives.

And it is only after the promised tour of Damascus and an elaborate lunch the next day that Georges makes the subtlest, most magnanimous of moves, delicately tracing her hands with his own, a slow accumulation of touch and taste that ends up in the grand king-sized bed in an Ottoman room, inhabited by Asfars, or so Dorle imagines, for generations.

Heavenly Words of Love

The earliest Asfar letter in Dorle's possession was
from April of 1935, three years after my flight of
fancy had taken her to Damascus. All the other
letters pick up the story in the midst of Dorle and
Georges's affair, beginning with Georges writing
from a France-bound ship after a disappointing
visit with Dorle. This first one tells little about
their relationship but exposes the basic tropes at
play between them.

Of men and women, of masters and mis-
tresses.

Georges, a Christian, instructs Dorle, a Jew,
on how to be a proper Muslim mistress.

Long before 9/11 and then Trump's ascen-
dance, "Mohammedanism" as it was often called,
must have conjured the romance of the Orient, the
exotic religion practiced in the land of *The Arabian
Nights*.

"I don't want you to take it for a reproach,"
Georges explains, "but your remark that woman
is the friend of the man just proves that you are a
stranger to the … giving, to the melting your will
and desire into one man's will."

"What you take as a slavery is a feeling
which will remain a stranger to you as long as
you consider yourself and your Master as two
persons … I don't blame you not to understand
these heavenly words of love … Have faith in
your Master. He will teach you the language. You
will join the chorus of these loves."

Dorle pores over these words, alarmed, enticed. Bill Barker could speak of cyclamens and sign off in Arabic, but only Georges could be her Oriental master.

The Golden Palace

Georges writes Dorle from a ship sailing from New York—where he has seen Dorle and watched a tremendous antiquities deal go south—to France en route to Syria. Like John Carter, like Bill Barker, he misses Dorle at sea. "I went to sleep this morning, Dorle. I feel like a lost lamb on this ship. I haunt the lounge to talk or look at anybody. I carried my chair to the front part of the ship and there for hours passed in review all what happened to me."

"The main reason of my heart broken was the disappointment I gave you. You went through certainly many dull, boring evenings waiting for me … I shall go back and first wash away any trace of Kevork from our mind, then I will start my work, live quietly and economically, plan and dream of what we shall do together. I love you, *habibi* [sweetheart]. Goodnight."

What happened—the disappointment—may have gone like this.

We know he went to New York to sell the Ottoman room now on display at the Metropolitan Museum to a wealthy patroness who wanted to build a museum of "Mohammedan" art in the Palisades: the expanse of sharp cliffs and sweeping views on the New Jersey side of the Hudson River where the Georges Washington Bridge had recently been built. The trip to America to arrange this tremendous sale had been planned as a romantic idyll for Georges and Dorle, but Georges's arch-nemesis, the Armenian antiquities merchant, Hagop Kevorkian ("Kevork"), had convinced the patroness to kill the deal.

The failed sale consumed Georges completely, eating up the time and energy he had planned to devote to Dorle.

Dorle waits for him one evening not long after the disaster at The Golden Pavilion, a Chinese restaurant a few blocks south of her apartment. The exterior is indeed shaped like a pavilion, a brilliant red and orange faux Chinese palace, clashing flamboyantly with the colorless office buildings, stores, and restaurants nearby. The interior is crammed with paper dragons, enormous vases, and waiters rushing back and forth with plates of chop suey, egg foo young and flaming pu pu platters. In a back booth lit by candles, Dorle finishes the martini she's been nursing for over an hour.

Georges's absence stings. So many men want to drink and dine with her, she reminds herself, while she's stuck waiting for this unreliable little man.

Who refuses to remove the spell he's cast upon her. He's given her three wishes like in the Aladdin story. Later letters suggest what they might be.

Her first is to show her the heart of the Orient —Bagdad, Cairo—the second involves carpets and jewels. The letter to her mother several years later, heralding the end of her relationship with John Carter, suggested that the third involved a greater intimacy between them that could only occur if he moved to New York. Though she had wanted to marry John, she had "never, I admit, been as emotionally close as I was to Georges."

Mobile phones will not start ringing for nearly seventy years, but somewhere in the back of the restaurant, Dorle hears the braying of a telephone. A moment later, one of the waiters in his Mandarin suit arrives to explain in a strong Chinese accent not particularly resembling Charlie Chan that the "gentleman not coming, Madam, big problem, emergency, gentleman very sorry."

She glares at the man for a few good seconds before trying to smile instead as there's no point in shooting the messenger.

Many Years Later

Towards the end of the nineties, my father is visiting Dorle in New York and has invited a younger colleague from the University of Virginia who he wants to impress, Tan Lin, the brother of Maya Lin. Angela and I have also been invited.

Nearly blind and growing more senile, Dorle is now cared for by Novelette Ewbanks, a woman from Jamaica who stayed with her from 1996 until Dorle's death in 2002.

My father decides that he would rather

not have Dorle join us for drinks. Explaining to Dorle about his visitor, he asks Novelette to serve Dorle's evening gin, tonic and Benson & Hedges in the living room on the other side of the large apartment and cook dinner for her afterwards.

Lin arrives. We have our drinks, and are preparing to walk across the street to a restaurant when Dorle's marvelously old-fashioned New York voice rings loudly and resonantly from the other side of the wall, "Is the Chinaman still here?"

Back on Ship

John Franklin Carter found a Dorle-like Jewess on the *Monarch of Bermuda*. Bill Barker turned a rose into Dorle when he traveled without her on the Lloyd Triestino Line. Later in the letter in which Georges Asfar apologizes for disappointing Dorle, he turns a cable she has sent him into an infant version of herself.

"I pushed your cable in my jacket, devoured my steak … took my baby round the deck for a long walk and had the best time. You fussed quite a bit when we headed to the windy upper deck, but I threatened to stop taking care of you if you are not an obedient girl."

For Georges, Dorle was an infant in grown woman form, flying in the face of her financially and sexually independent New York life to accept the role of docile Oriental mistress, turning him (so mild-mannered looking in his picture) into the powerful figure of an Oriental man.

For John, she was the Jewess-cum-beast, fucking with animal abandon, fighting with animal fierceness.

For the simpler (though not simple-minded) Bill Barker, Dorle was a siren singing to the men at her dining table on the Lloyd Triestino Line, the woman who broke his heart by refusing, in the end, to be swayed by deserts and cyclamen.

For each man in turn, Dorle represented some anomalous feminine trope, standing out amidst the broads and ladies. Wild, but seducible, she allowed them to take on their own desired masculine personae: John, the important man of the world; Georges, the Oriental Master. But none could have strolled so confidently across a movie screen as Bill Barker, risking his life in Gallipoli, Dublin, Palestine.

Later in the evening, when loud jazz drives Georges out onto the deck, he leaves Dorle's cable behind to continue his fantasy of her: not wild animal but vulnerable infant, needing his protection.

"I do not dare take you out for a walk. It is so windy and cold. I cannot keep you in the reading room, the trepidation is awful, so, my Dorle, I leave you alone in your bed."

Verb Tense

"I left Paris by train to Damascus. My mind all the time was flying from New York to Damascus.

Every time a beautiful sight was in view I was thrilled at the idea that you and I will be together there. I watched the narrow dangerous zigzag car road through Asia Minor and dreamed of a thousand and one incidents we had in our crossing."

"Incidents we had" is a tense slip-up. He means "will have," as he's plotting Dorle's next trip to the Orient.

Politics: *Les Arabes*

When Georges reaches Damascus, where he must wait for several months for Dorle to visit, he discusses the political situation in the Middle East and the world at large.

In the Middle East at that time, the British were trying to settle Jews into their Palestinian colony while suppressing Arab resistance, and a larger pan-Arabic movement was picking up steam, Syria itself soon to be liberated from the French. But where does that leave Georges, a well-heeled Christian who did most of his business with westerners?

A friend who is part of the longstanding Syrian/Lebanese Christian community in Brooklyn has always felt kinship with the Palestinian struggle, viewing Palestinians as fellow Arabs. When she visited her Lebanese relatives in Beirut for the first time, she was shocked to discover their enmity towards Muslim Arabs, particularly Palestinians.

We see something of this in Georges eighty

years before.

"After the Syrians obtain their complete independence ... I don't think the Christians can possibly live here. They will be always subject to a sudden uprising endangering their lives. The *surexcitation* [agitation] of the Moslems is reaching every day a new height. Unless the government is wise to allow the Jews to settle in Syria, Syria will be a ruin economically in the very near future, and depression and miseries are responsible for the wave of *fanatisme* raging all over the Moslem countries now."

Politics: *Les Juives*

When Georges wishes the "government" would allow in Jews and warns of financial disaster if they don't, he may be trying to win the sympathy of his Jewish mistress, but he also suggests that "Balfour gave [the Jews] Palestine to get their money and used the German Jews against the German nation during the war. They tried and obtained from a German Jew the gag asphyxiate used in the German army."

Not a very flattering view of the Jews. But Georges's next letter doesn't mention it, so Dorle does not appear to have objected.

But why was she silent?

When an evil general in Costa-Gavras's *Z* disparages a Jewish insurgent and is reminded that the man was only half Jewish, he declares that halves were worss because they considered

137

themselves superior. My own half-Jewish discon-
nect takes us too far astray, but it's worth noting
that Dorle, Dario, and Faie were not very Jewish
Jews, particularly when it came to the Holocaust,
an event which occurred when they were in early
middle age. Even though Dario came to America
from Italy to flee it, the only time I remember anything like it being brought up is the strange case
of Uncle Arturo. An ostensibly funny family story
has the implicitly gay Arturo just not getting how
serious it was to be imprisoned by the fascists and
trying to send for his manservant to bring along
his dressing gown.

It's a long journey psychically as well as geo-
graphically from German and eastern European
Jews on transports to Auschwitz and Dachau to
Dario, the son of another Jewish banking family
that lost their fortune, leaving Rome with some
money and very nice clothes, to seek his fortune
while his parents and all other relatives that I'm
aware of survived the war back in Italy. (Eighty
percent of Italian Jews survived the Holocaust,
and I'm sure the wealthier you were, the easier
that got.) But even that PG-rated Holocaust sur-
vival must have had its own taste of terror.

A lovely, pine-cone-shaped, red plush ottoman made it all the way from Dario's parents' Roman apartment to Brooklyn.

I imagine Dario's parents seated upon it one
afternoon towards the end of the thirties.

Dario's two trunks are packed, and he
wears a light summer suit appropriate for a July
ocean-crossing.

His parents aren't going with him to Naples where he will board the SS *Conte Grande* to New York, a ship that will be requisitioned by the US Navy several years later after the war has started and Italy has been defeated.

Because that would make the farewell harder to bear.

When he'd shipped off to Eritrea with the Italian army five or six years before, the atmosphere had been so much lighter. There was always danger in a long journey to a colonial territory, but Asmara was firmly in Italian hands, and the lives of Italian Jews back in Italy were safe, comfortable, and in many cases prosperous.

But an ominous rumbling can be felt just about everywhere by the Sorias and their friends now that Mussolini has bonded with Hitler, and a not-too-distant threat can be easily imagined. The family conversations have involved opportunity rather than danger, the great possibilities available for an ambitious young man in the United States and the dwindling ones at home. What's happening to Jews over the German border has been more silently fretted upon than openly discussed, but the tension is palpable.

So when Dario hugs his parents goodbye before beginning the short journey to Naples in order to launch the long one to New York, they cling to each other for longer than before.

A Carpet Tale

Back in 1936, the time of our story, Dorle returns from a long day of work to find a much more amusing letter with nothing about Arabs or Jews. She laughs buoyantly at an incredible story of the rug business with a dramatis personae including Erich Remarque, the writer of *All Quiet on the Western Front*, and King Edward the VIII of Britain.

The division into acts is Georges's, not my own.

Act One

Georges plans to sell a carpet for a relatively cheap price to an unnamed woman, as he is desperate "to realize cash." When he somehow learns that the woman plans to sell the carpet to Remarque, who, in turn, plans to sell it to King Edward for three times the price, he calls off the deal. The woman offers to split the profit of the Remarque resale, but Georges refuses.

Act Two

The same woman finds "a wealthy friend … to Flandrin, the French Minister who knows full well Remarque who is going to give the price offered by these dealers and sell to Remarque or directly to Edward VIII and share the profit." Georges proceeds to accept basically the same offer he rejected in Act One. Act Two also features a diatribe against Calouste Gulbenkian, another member of Georges's least favorite tribe, the Armenians.

Act Three

In the not very dramatic final act, Asfar goes "quite often to the shop of this woman [the one from Act One and Two] who has a charming husband, and the two are very fond of me, and every word they told me after examination was the very truth."

Syria again:
The Hunt for Gazelles

When Dorle finally arrived back in Syria, she and Georges went on a gazelle hunt.

"Before I started," she wrote her mother, *"the idea was dreadful to me. Gazelles were beautiful and to hunt them in cars not particularly sportsmanlike. But it turned out to be most exciting. In fact I found out later that I was lucky in two ways—first to be taken along as there are often accidents and women are apt to be a nuisance, second to have had the luck to see two herds as often trips are made for nothing. We left at three in the morning from Damascus with a friend of Georges's and a great sportsman, the head of the Bank of Syria here. At four, we arrived at a small Arab village, the property of Hussein Bey Ibisch. Ibisch is a famous hunter. Every year he goes with his friend, Prince Joseph Kamal of Egypt, to India or the Sudan for big game and his collection of trophies is being made into a museum. His family had been active in politics for generations, but he has retired to this village where he lives a semi-feudal life very typical of many parts of Syria. There we left Georges's closed car and changed*

to a dilapidated open one, specially adapted for hunting, with a floor stained brown with old blood. In the back were Georges and me. On the two small seats in the far back with guns ready were two Bedouins. The driver's job is the most difficult. You must know the land thoroughly, be an expert hunter so as to search out the gazelles and anticipate their movements and be able to drive under the most trying conditions. We went for about a half hour or so from the village until we were in the midst of the Hamad, not actually the desert but a large belt of semi-arid land outside of Damascus. During the day the gazelles stay in the Wahr or rocky parts surrounding the Hamad but at dawn come down into the planes [sic] to sip the dew off the bits of grass and small scattered shrubs. It is forbidden by law to hunt them and there is a fine of 125.00 for every animal you are found with, but Ibisch is a law unto himself in this particular section.

The air was very fresh, quite cold, and there was a wind. Even close the gazelles are hard to see as they are white with tan markings and easily camouflaged by the stones and bits of dried grass. We drove about for a while. Here and there taking our direction for reasons I couldn't understand. Orders were to kill only males.

Suddenly a herd was spotted far off in the distance, like rabbits. Off we went at breakneck speed. Gazelles, before they are tired, run at 75 kilometers an hour. The herd divided, one was shot, the other finally outdistanced us. By this time, it was almost six o'clock, usually too late to hunt. However we kept on, finally after ten or fifteen minutes wandering about, one of the Bedouins shouted. I looked in the direction indicated. The Arabs have extraordinary eyesight because it was *not until we had driven for at least three or four minutes that I could, with the greatest difficulty, make out small moving spots far away.*

The car went mad. In front of me, the Bedouin stood up, swaying back and forth with the movement of the car, his gun cocked. I was thrown left and right. I hung desperately to my seat and to Georges and was knocked black and blue. But in the excitement, I never noticed anything. The Arabs shouted contradictory directions: right—left—straight ahead. Only a man of Ibisch's experience could have kept his head. With drivers of less concentration, accidents often happen. Cars upset, guns go off in the wrong direction.

We neared the herd, they ran like the wind in front of us. We finally shot five, three escaped much to the Arabs' chagrin. The chase over, we turned back, with difficulty retracing the path the car had taken, to find the gazelles we had shot as we went. Each time we stopped, the Bedouin got out of the car, turned the head of the dying gazelle south towards Mecca and slit its throat. When we got back to the village, the Arabs took out the entrails of the animals, then brought them to a great stone in the middle of the Khan or courtyard where the sheep are kept during the night. The stone looked like a primitive sacrificial altar. There the gazelles were cleaned with water. We were back at the hotel by nine o'clock. We took one gazelle with us. I will bring you the antlers. We ate the gazelle the next day. I didn't want to but Georges is impatient with my sentimentalities so I tasted it. The meat originally is dry but good. It was prepared with wine, much like a rabbit, and so disguised that I didn't recognize it as a gazelle and liked it very much.

Palmrya

"There was a French Countess," Dorle wrote her mother from Palmyra, "who came to this country, divorced her husband, married a Moslem in order to go to Mecca, finally poisoned her Arab husband and was condemned to death. But meanwhile she had acquired [a] hotel in Palmyra, which is the French military centre in the desert. At that time there was a rule that no officer might marry and so the modern Zenobia ruled without rival over the entire garrison. When she was sentenced, she seduced the judges one by one and all the officers swore to defend her. So finally, she was retried and the case eventually dropped."

Dorle described Palmyra, as "a ruined city of the third century in the heart of the desert … Some 1700 years ago Palmyra was a great city where caravans coming from Bagdad and from Damascus went and exchanged goods. Now there is nothing left but ruins of enormous temples and low rows of broken columns showing where the city streets had been."

In a snapshot of Georges and Dorle at Palmyra that somehow landed in the Library of Congress archives, they hold hands in the desert, Roman columns lying behind them.

Dorle stands erect, energetic and determined. Her mouth is slightly ajar, revealing the tips of her teeth: a wry, sphinx-like half-smile. It is her expression of appreciation. She employs it

144

when she listens to people she admires or watches theater or opera. Of course, she smiles like that while standing with her Oriental lover under the hard Oriental sun.

At first glance, Georges looks worried, unsure how things are working out, but a closer look reveals that the sun is in his eyes, part of the reason for the tension in his face. His mouth also looks ajar, a version of a smile, but mostly he is dazed. Dorle has returned. The event he's spent months preparing for is finally underway.

Time Travel:
A Horror Movie

Of course, reading Dorle's letters to her mother and her lovers' letters to Dorle sent me back and forth between my present and Dorle's past.

As I read about Palmyra in recent times and go through the tourist postcards Dorle brought back from there eighty-odd years ago, I can't stop myself from sending her on a sadistic voyage.

Dorle—curious, explorative, unlikely to stick with any lover or guide—slips behind a nearby Roman temple because she hears a peculiar mechanical sound.

In back of the temple, the sun shines in her eyes, she wipes them, blinks, but the strange scene remains in front of her. Men in black clothes with black veils over their heads and black scarves over their mouths, wearing unfathomable twenty-first century running shoes, carry objects over their shoulders that resemble rifles. Some cluster silently in groups as if they don't know what to do with themselves. Others apply massive machines to drill their way through a temple that Dorle and Georges had only just seen, bits of it falling off onto the ground.

I'll pull Dorle back to Georges in 1934 before she sees the decapitated body of an archaeologist and becomes somehow visible herself and subject to however ISIS would treat the sudden appearance of a white western woman in inconceivably old-fashioned clothes.

The Return to Damascus

Georges drives Dorle to Haifa, where she picks up another Lloyd Triestino craft to begin her long voyage back to the United States.

Later he describes his own journey back to Damascus.

"I left Haifa as a drunk man, my foot on the gas clutch was trembling. I started out with the feeling all the time that I was on the wrong road. I knew there was only one road, but everything looked so different to me." Potent and disorienting, the Dorle experience scrambles familiar terrains.

Georges wishes trouble upon himself in order to have a more dramatic tale to tell to Dorle. At the frontier, mandate Palestine, "the man kept me waiting for more than twenty minutes looking over and over my passport. … It's the only time

I didn't mind to be arrested with a false passport … it would have been the climax of our romance. I was pleading that my love for you brought me to use a false passport when suddenly the officer wakes me up from my dream and handed me my passport."

Once back in Damascus, poor Georges can only go through the motions. "Everyone is nice with me here. I boast with false cheerfulness to be the same, but I am afraid that I am not such a good comedian."

That stunning adventure with its ancient ruins, gazelle hunts, hotels run by Arab-poisoning femme fatales, and probably incredible fucking has come and gone, and all that remains is his torpid old life. Dorle's passion for the Middle East imbued familiar vistas with exotic charm, but in her absence, Damascus seems just dull and chaotic as Syria's political uncertainty groans on.

New York

Georges's next letter introduces a topic that will dominate their correspondence, Dorle's apparent insistence that he decamp to New York.

I had been skeptical, at first, when John talked of Dorle's determination for him to leave his wife. The fearless elderly Dorle I'd known as a child and younger adult; the Dorle of much of these letters, waltzing around the globe "curing love with love;" even the adolescent Dorle of her diaries, tough-minded about the inevitable course of human affection, just didn't seem like the same woman who hedged her bets by begging not only Georges but also John to uproot themselves for her. In my last days in Dorle's apartment before it was cleared out and sold, I sat at her desk in the company of her furniture and her filing cabinets and tried to picture her going back and forth to work at Columbia Artists, sailing by herself to Europe and the Middle East, enjoying a freedom that the letters from John and from Georges suggested she was desperate to surrender. In Georges's letters, Dorle's neediness began to seem incontrovertible, her words to her mother about how close she'd felt to him suggesting it all the more. No genie had magically dissolved the social and emotional pressures to find a man.

One New Year's Eve when Dorle was well into her nineties, surrounded by my parents, Angela, and myself, she opened the art deco dining room window just a crack and was disappointed not to hear the sounds of celebration. Even surrounded by her family, she seemed lonely and a little bit bored.

"So many times these last months, I have been to war to leave ... and always fast at the last moment I was forced to give up this trip," Georges tells her.

"My Dorle I miss you every day more and more. I think all the time what could be the possibilities of changing actual conditions. Leaving Damascus to run away to NY would be throwing my firm in a great mess."

What if Georges gets past his business troubles and leaves Damascus just as John is ditching his job and his wife? Quite a pickle for Dorle, a scene out of a comic opera, John hiding in the closet while Georges bursts in through the door.

These must have been stressful times for Dorle, though, having strong feeling about two men, neither of whom could fully commit to her. I was relieved to read her letter to her mother about them because it revealed she had at least one confidante. In the years that I knew her long past her mother's death, she lacked close female friends. Once Dorle said something to my mother that she found hurtful and scoffed when my mother cried. People, particularly women, were not supposed to admit weakness.

I can still hear Dorle clearing her throat dismissively after someone praised her for succeeding professionally in an era in which few women did. Now, I wonder if she'd forgotten how contemptuous her father had been of her own journalistic ambition. Perhaps she just viewed it as par for the course. Days could be too hot or too cold, dogs bark, men could be difficult. One succeeded despite rather than because of them.

The mantle of feminism fit her awkwardly. A complex concoction of strength and insecurity, Dorle pooh-poohed the struggles of women and probably wasn't kidding about them being nuisances on gazelle hunts.

As for her master lovers, both real and fictional, they came from different locales and cultures but had one thing in common—strength

149

and dominance. She would have it no other way.

Interlude:
Master Harasser

Dorle told several tales of famous conductors of her day that hinted of sex, malice, or both. When George Szell tossed hot peppers on her face, according to legend, Dario got out an old family sword. Somehow, she found herself driving through Mexico with Fritz Reiner, who laughed uncontrollably at every sign that said "curva" because apparently it meant whore in his native Hungarian.

Recently, my father told me a story born for the #MeToo era about another conductor, Otto Klemperer, whose son would play Colonel Klink on *Hogan's Heroes*. One look at Klemperer's beaky face makes it painful to imagine him chasing Dorle around her desk at her office at Columbia Artists, trying to pin her down and assault her.

But she was lithe enough to escape, and Klemperer was not rewarded (like Spacey, Lauer et al.) with humiliation and termination from his post at the Los Angeles Philharmonic. Dorle would have been laughed out of town had she made a fuss about such common male behavior, so she played it for laughs, turning the incident into comic cocktail party fodder.

Some Strange Lost Gender

Dorle was in the middle of her eighties, very much in her prime, when her grandnephew (me) landed at a hippie, nudist vegetarian co-op at Oberlin College. Now, decades on, I imagine what would have happened if she'd visited me.

She strolls the halls with her stick, what she called her cane, peering at the peculiar, long-haired, desperately sensitive men. Their exposed junk and bizarre attire don't bother her terribly, but their mode of masculinity confounds. Not fighting Franco, hunting gazelles, or conducting symphonies, they huddle in silly circles on the grass, strumming discordantly on guitars. Not proper men or women, some strange lost gender.

Dorle must have gone about her days during the difficult period when Georges was back in Damascus and John busy with FDR in Washington: her meetings with musicians and businessmen; her dinners with her mother and her sister; her concerts and her cocktail parties, bearing a secret sadness. You could catch it at stray moments. A solitary tear creeps down her face at her office at Columbia Artists. Her shoulders sink after Georges's latest missive deflects the idea of coming to New York. Her smile collapses, and she places her head in her hands while a supercilious conductor is in the bathroom during a dreary business lunch, only to buoy herself back up again when he returns as one has to make a show.

Transparency

When Georges next writes Dorle, nearly a year has passed with no concrete plan for the two of them to see each other, and Georges speaks frankly about his interest in prostitutes.

"Fouaz proposed to cheer me up to take me to a Pazon ... The adventure would have amused me if you were with me; bring back a concubine, I would have loved to watch your reaction; but a concubine behaves so well toward the legitimate wife, that I am sure you would have been enchanted."

John Carter wrote of Dorle "curing love with love" when she disclosed her intention to see other men. Carter complains about "Mr. Asfar," and his "hashish cigarettes" letting us know that Dorle had revealed with whom she planned to be curing it with. And in the same letter in which Georges talks about prostitutes, we learn that Dorle has told him about Bill Barker.

"It seems to me, Dorle, that your policeman in Palestine is quite assiduous in his correspondence with you. I must call on him one day." Georges's declaration that "others too worry my heart" suggests that he knows that Bill is not her only other lover.

Georges, himself, is strikingly transparent about his own struggles with fidelity. "I confess to you, Dorle, that never before in my life I have enjoyed the pleasure of being faithful (even though it was relative faithfulness in the beginning!)." Such candor and tolerance come as a surprise from a man in the 1930s who had suggested his mistress take on the submissive role of an "Oriental" wife.

New York, Again

Dorle and Georges continue to write back and forth about the possibility of his moving to New York.

If the American courts rule in Kevorkian's favor, Georges's immense sale of antiquities for the museum of Islamic art may go through, and his pockets will be lined with gold. But if they do not, it would be nearly impossible to transplant a struggling antiquities business from the Damascus medina to New York.

Did the older Dorle ever look back at herself in her thirties and wonder why she found John and Georges so hard to give up, why she pushed them that hard? Georges never makes Dorle promises in his letters, but he may have in person.

I see them on their last night in Damascus, twisted together between cool satin sheets under a whirring ceiling fan, tipsy from drinking, flushed from fucking.

How would he have put it? "Dorle, my darling. I promise you … Before the year has passed, I shall … You have rubbed the brass bottle and the genie will grant your wish."

In any case, the Kevorkian business stands firmly in the way. John Carter encouraged the mysterious use of Armenian code to communicate with Dorle under Sheila's radar while the nefarious doings of an actual Armenian keep her from Georges, whose next letter already has something of a valedictory tone. "*Je vous dois tous le success de ces jours,*" he says, wishing her success for the rest of her days as if they were unlikely to include him.

The Verdict

By the next time he writes, the verdict is in.

"The question to be decided by the Court was must the court of Syria inquire into the merit of the N.Y. court judging or not; the decision comes out ... It will be too long to write to you the detail of this judgment, but it was a shock to everyone and contrary to our laws; Kevorkian has planned this judgment as a general plans a battle."

Asfar's hope that the case be brought back to a Syrian court has been dashed, leaving the Kevorkian affair a devastating defeat. The *New York Times* describes the verdict as follows:

> *A judgment for $50,046 filed in Supreme Court in favor of Hagop Kevorkian, collector of Mohammedan art objects, against Asfar and Sarkis, dealers in Islamic art objects at Damascus, Syria, has disclosed an unusual litigation over the importation of the two interiors that Mr. Kevorkian, as the buyer, was justified in canceling the contracts for the houses on the grounds of misrepresentation.*

"I have all the time so vivid and intense the memories of my happiness with you. I don't know if I can ever get interested in any other woman ... I love you, Dorle, as much as any time before."

At her desk one morning a few weeks later, Dorle rereads Georges's letter as well as the *Times* story about the verdict, more melancholy than distressed. How strange that a little story in the morning paper could change both of their lives. She had already suspected that the verdict would go against Georges, and even if it didn't, she wasn't sure he would fulfill his promise and move to New York. She is nearing forty, and men have promised her many things. Now, she won't have to approach Mother about marrying either a New England or Syrian gentile, a silver lining of a sort.

On July 5th, Georges writes what will be his last letter for several decades.

"I am sorry, Dorle, to tell you that in this time we lost our poor Papa; his second attack of angina in his chest surprised him during his convalescence. He was too weak to survive it; it is the first time in my life that I realize the meaning of the loss of a person who one holds dear."

Which may actually sting, as he has recently lost another, Dorle, who'd had every reason to think she'd been held dear.

Flashing Forward

Dorle and Dario sit in their living room on 55th Street one evening in the middle of the 1970s watching the six o'clock news with Walter Cronkite. Vietnam is a few years past, but strife from around the world still appears and disappears on the state-of-the-art television that RCA gave Dario, safely contained inside its imposing screen.

Except the following has arrived from Georges. Around the time of Syrian independence in the forties, he had moved his family and business to Beirut. Now civil war has driven him from Lebanon.

"You must be surprised to learn that we are all living in Paris, since last June, when bombing and insecurity became unbearable … You probably heard that the St. George Hotel and our shops were looted by the Palestinians, and burned, thank God, most of our precious antiquities and rugs were put away some time before."

Dorle sits with her drink across from Dario, hears the rattle of gunfire and flinches when a bomb explodes a building.

"Georges" slips from her mouth.

And Dario looks across at her, remembers the man forced from Lebanon who was once his wife's lover and sighs sympathetically while Nancy Walker selling Bounty replaces Lebanon on the screen.

Georges's next letter brings us full circle as it involves the installation of Georges's Ottoman room in the Metropolitan Museum.

The Kevorkian defeat still rankles decades later.

"Thank you for the Metropolitan publication about the 'Nouriddine Room' as it's called by the Museum. 'Nouriddine' is the name of the owner and Kevorkian during the trial objected that I misled him by calling the room 'Nouriddine'. It's the name of a very famous Arabic warrior in the past!! ... *Ce monde est vraiment bien bizarre.*"

Georges's final letter to Dorle in 1980 condoles her for the loss of Dario.

"*Du Courage ma chére Dorle, et souhaite nous encore a nous beaucoup de courage, J'espère qui ou passera ensemble a Paris l'année prochaine ... Je t'embrace très fort.*"

Sending her a firm embrace, he tells her to have courage, what Dorle and Dario themselves would say to those who'd lost loved ones, using *coragio*, the Italian word.

Georges hopes they can meet each other in Paris, and I like to imagine that they did.

Following her and Bill Barker's now very old footprints, she leads him from Montmartre to Notre Dame, one of her favorite walks.

Old landmarks and new restaurants rescue their conversation when it lapses, and Dorle periodically glances over at the weathered, round face of the 73-year-old Georges, remembering her determination to bring him back to New York.

Of course, his obsession with the perfidious Kervorkian, now fourteen years dead, comes up in conversation.

They are crossing the Pont Neuf over to the Île de la Cité just as Georges's harangue finally closes. He catches Dorle's eye. His face flushes. His eyes dart bashfully downward.

"It was no lie," he suddenly declares in

French as if he stands accused, "if Kevork had lost, I would have gone to New York. You would have had to tell your mother you were marrying a Christian."

Dorle smiles warmly, imagining the very different life she would have led. Looking over at Georges and recalling her magnificent Dario, she feels grateful, for a treacherous moment, to Kevorkian for taking Georges away from her.

Guilty about that thought, she grabs Georges's hands and pumps it with her own, a gesture bound to be misinterpreted.

CHAPTER EIGHT
THE BOYS

While Dorle was visiting George in Syria, the men who would become her closest companions in her last years of life were experiencing very different boyhoods in New York and in Italy. Floriano Vecchi capered in the streets of Bologna, an adorable blond *scugnizzo*, that terrific Neapolitan word for the pre-pubescent boy scoundrels skirmishing in neorealist movies. And Tobias Schneebaum was drawing abstract street scenes and devouring Errol Flynn at the movies while living with his working-class Jewish family in the largely Scandinavian world of Bay Ridge, Brooklyn.

In his 1958 memoir, *Keep the River on Your Right*, Tobias describes leaving an inhospitable beatnik-era New York where his queer desires went unfulfilled for that gay-friendly mecca, 1950s Peru. He found his way from Cuzco to an isolated Catholic mission. From there he walked for days along a river farther into the jungle, where he was initiated into a tribe that had had no prior contact with the outside world in which male bisexuality was the norm. Almost immediately, he met the first of a lifetime of indigenous lovers.

One morning after a month or two of living with the tribe, Tobias was awakened excruciatingly early. All men, save the elders, were required to walk for hours until they reached a rival village and engaged in a killing spree.

Tobias stuck his spear into a corpse to participate without actually murdering anyone, and took at least one bite of their human meal, a taste that would permanently unnerve him.

Several decades before, Tobias's parents had immigrated separately from one Sender Jarmulowsky territory to another: eastern Poland to the Lower East Side. But they never lost money in the Jarmulowsky bank, at least, not according to the story of Tobias's parents' early life as told in Tobias's second book, *Wild Man*.

His father sold eggs from a cart, and his mother worked maintenance for several buildings on the block, "carrying up and down cans of ash and garbage." Tobias assumed that a matchmaker had introduced them as their miserable-sounding marriage was clearly no love match. The day after Tobias was born, his mother was back at work, a different type of labor.

When Tobias was four, his parents bought a small grocery store and moved to Brooklyn. A few years later, Tobias was radically transformed by an encounter with "The Wild Man of Borneo" freak show at Coney Island.

"Half man, half ape, human or orangutan," he wrote, "the presence of him startled and confused me, and filled me with the wildness of his look. He took hold of me, captured me and turned my insides on end … that creature rattling around my heart and brain … visions of him loaded me with terror, longing and excitement."

This romanticized vision of "primitive" man doesn't seem far afield from the sentimentalized stories about Casanova, Henry VIII, et al. that Dorle was penning at about that same time.

Dorle, in fact, was an admirer of Tobias years before he became a regular figure in her life. Towards the end of the 1970s, Dorle took me to see him speak at the Asia Society in Manhattan. Dorle beamed as he revealed the way in which men in Asmat greeted each other by waving their penises. And about a year later, she listened sympathetically to a story that shocked my callow adolescent self about an African American hustler who had been sent to Attica when his john died in the midst of S&M play of the john's devising. In Tobias's heteronormative (to say the least) 1930s Jewish world, a man having sex with any man was inconceivable much less the Wild Man of Borneo.

"My youthful years were agonizing," he wrote. "I felt a need to hold the wild man, to touch and taste him."

Hence his escape to Peru.

To which Tobias reluctantly returned in the 1990s when David and Laurie Shapiro made a film about Tobias, named *Keep the River on Your Right* after his book, and wanted to film him revisiting his old haunts.

In Peru, he manages to find what he thinks is his tribe, but they have been pushed out of the jungle into small-town squalor. They claim to have never been cannibals, and I began to wonder, as I watched the movie, if they were really the same people, or if Tobias's whole story was some sort of fantasy—until he shows the elders photos of their ancestors, and they are moved beyond comprehension.

Tobias also returns to Asmat where he shares a heart-wrenching canoe ride with another indigenous man who had also been his lover. Physically, they almost resembled each other. Tobias's craggy Jewish nose and deeply imbedded tan made him look South Asian maybe, hardly the white Jewish Brooklyn man that he really was.

At Yaddo, where Tobias was a regular for years, at museums, luxury anthropological cruises and dinner parties, he would play tribal Asmat instruments and sing and dance Asmat dances: his body awkward and shaky, his Brooklyn accent loud and clear, a magically transcultural experience for those who were lucky enough to witness it.

Tobias's indigenous lovers never visited the United States, but I met several non-indigenous ones. Douglas from New Zealand was a member of the Paul Taylor Dance Company. Tobias, bad hip and all, played a convincing elderly canine in Douglas's ballet, *Dog Dance*. My memory had it that Douglas (like so many of Tobias and Floriano's friends) had been dying of AIDS, but I looked him up recently and learned he had returned to Auckland and lived until 2018.

Tobias's last lover, Joel, was about thirty years his junior. He had cared for his previous elderly lover until the lover's death and planned, I think, to do the same for Tobias, who was

162

failing both physically and cognitively as the aughts moved on and his Parkinson's took hold.

But when Joel fell in love with someone younger rather than older, Tobias shrugged it off. From the Wild Man of Borneo to lovers, indigenous and otherwise, he'd experienced too much to be phased. And did not wish to ruin his limited time left on earth with bitterness or grief.

Tobias was large, craggy, blunt. Floriano, delicate, elegant, wispy. I don't think they were ever lovers, but as the years went by and so many of their friends died, they developed an extraordinary intimacy, a sort of duality. I cannot remember one without thinking of the other.

I know little about Floriano's youth because, unlike Tobias, he published no memoirs. He was born in Bologna, but by his early twenties (he once told me) he was riding around Rome on the back of Marcello Mastroianni's Vespa.

He met his great love, an American named Richard Miller, at the University of Rome in 1949. Soon, they moved to New York where they founded the Tiber Press in 1953. Tiber (which Floriano ran until 1977) printed art by latter-day abstract expressionists such as Alfred Leslie and Helen Frankenthaler along with Ben Shahn and Georgia O'Keefe. They also published the early poetry of John Ashbury, James Merrill, and Frank O'Hara.

More significant to the art world was the visit the young Andy Warhol made to the Tiber offices in 1962. He had an idea for a dollar bill print, but needed Floriano to teach him to silk screen. Hence Mao. Hence Marilyn.

Dorle met Tobias and Floriano through their close friend, William Weaver, a young American hired to translate libretti for their Cetra-Soria label.

Bill, who'd learned Italian by staying in Italy after driving an ambulance during the war, would go on to translate *The Name of the Rose* and other works by Umberto Ecco and Italo Calvino.

In the 1970s, Bill made Dorle an honorary female member of *circolo*, a circle of gay men that included Floriano living in the hills above the small Tuscan town of Monte San Savino. Though he may have visited, Tobias of the huge nose and dubious anthropology, was never a real member of *circolo*, which had started to fade by the eighties.

Floriano sold his house there near the end of that decade. But he continued to travel back and forth to Italy to visit his brother and his closest friend, a detective for the art police. During that time, Tobias spent a month or so annually as a guide on a cruise ship to Indonesia and Papua New Guinea on which Mick Jagger was once a passenger.

But by the mid-1990s, Floriano's brother and his art cop friend had died, and he and Tobias were both slowing down. By the end of the decade, they only really traveled regularly from their Village apartments to Dorle.

Dorle, too, was fading, losing her sight, hearing, and short-term memory. Tobias and Floriano were (along with Benson & Hedges and gin

164

and tonics) among her few remaining pleasures.

To visit Dorle in the last years of her life would not have been at all the same. Greeting her guests had been a grand event. Dorle would listen carefully for the bell before pausing to compose herself, then rushing towards the door.

But by late-1990s, she no longer cared particularly, even if she hadn't been too deaf to hear it. Novelette would let guests in, and they would find Dorle sitting quietly by herself, slowing sipping her Bombay Gin and tonic, watered down as not to further disable her faculties, and puffing distractedly on her cigarettes. She kept up those primal pleasures, but they no longer particularly pleased her.

Like an old dog wishing to be left alone, she didn't particularly appreciate my screams into her ears when I came over, my attempts to engage her briefer and briefer moments of short-term memory.

September 11 happened a few months before she died, and I tried to explain it. She grasped the planes. She grasped the towers. But not the former crashing into the latter.

On one of my last visits to Dorle, I hugged her hello.

And she stiffened.

"Leave me be," she demanded. Her voice strong, her conviction clear.

The most regular visitors to apartment 8B were, of course, the boys. Floriano, frail, delicate, as beautiful as ever and Tobias, his gawky companion, spoke softly into her ears. She'd actually smile. Sometimes, she'd laugh.

What would they have spoken of? Perhaps, they spoke of love. If Dorle had entrusted anyone with the secrets of her polyamorous 1930s, the tales told in letters hidden in nooks and crannies surrounding them, it would have been them. As brave gay men of their era, born a century before marriage equality, when queer love was punishable by law, they would hardly have been troubled by a little marital infidelity.

Floriano was faithful in body and spirit for the last decades of his life to Richard Miller, who'd died in a car wreck in the seventies. Tobias may not have been particularly faithful to anyone but was honest and forthright with his many lovers.

Dorle's real master lovers were too worldly to allow anything to shock them. One evening in the early sixties, according to a Floriano story sadly lost to time, W. H. Auden spoke eagerly to his fellow guests of the dancing of sphincter muscles.

I remember the look of distrust, distaste, on my mother's face when Floriano told us the story, and Dorle's broad smile.

It was Tobias and Floriano who adjudicated the terrible dispute between Dorle and my mother that occurred when my parents hired someone to care for Dorle.

When Dorle started to really grow old, slowly disappearing into deafness, blindness, and senility, my father found it painful to spend time with her. But my mother, approaching old age

herself, came every other month, flying or training from what felt like exile in Charlottesville to
the city that ran deep in her veins.

At the beginning of the 1950s when she
was in her early twenties, my mother had left
her working class Czech immigrant family in
Cleveland for New York, and the city remained
a precious life force, an emblem of glamour and
sophistication that matched the more and more
elaborate clothes and jewels she wore as she grew
older.

By 1996, my mother's Parkinson's was
worsening, and Dorle was finally, truly, aging. It
was a classic story: gas burners left on, water running in her bathtub. Something had to be done to
save apartment 8B from fire or flood.

Money wasn't really an issue. The trouble was pride. And probably some sickly sixth
sense that once she let her independence slip, it
would keep slipping until it was gone altogether.
Better to have her apartment blown up by gas
than turned into a cage.

My father, her closest relative, flew up to
New York. Sitting her down and summoning his
most dour and masculine tone, he gravely announced that she could no longer live alone.

He returned home satisfied. She appeared
to accept it. She appeared to understand.

But soon afterwards we received word from
the boys. Dorle was in the grips of some cataclysmic rage. My mother, the only other woman in
Dorle's circle, had been scapegoated. Novelette,
the caretaker, had intruded on her life, and it was

all my mother's fault.

I wasn't there. I didn't see it. But I have to stop romanticizing Dorle to imagine it. She shakes her fist. She stamps her feet. Her angry voice cascades through the apartment. Some of the fury tasted by John Franklin Carter half a century before had been shaken loose into the air.

And with it came a terrible edict. My mother had been banned. While the betrayal came at the hands of her nephew, his wife would never be allowed back in her apartment.

But New York was everything to my mother, Dorle's New York, Dorle's apartment, nothing any hotel or other friend could provide. So my mother and I had made a careful plan. She was to arrive around six in the evening from Virginia, and I was to get to Dorle's apartment just ahead of her to buffer, to troubleshoot, and, if necessary, to help my mother move to the moderately priced hotel across the street.

Agonizingly, the F train got stuck around Rockefeller Center, then crawled so slowly towards the station that by the time I'd climbed up to the street it was after six. My mother might already have arrived and been dismissed, ejected.

I rang the bell and was let in by my mother to witness a quiet melancholy scene. The two women sat across from each other, Dorle smoking and drinking gin, my mother breathing heavily and gratefully, her hand shaking more than ever, the edict tacitly withdrawn.

CHAPTER NINE
"THE MYSTERIES OF JOANNY"

If Dorle's novice lover, Albert Coates, the composer and conductor, could have been associated with one of Dorle's master lovers, he would have probably chosen Franz Liszt: "A virtuoso who shook the world with the mad glory of his music. A philanderer with flowing hair and piercing blue eyes."

While trying to piece together Coates's time with Dorle, I would find myself in a tricky situation. I would need to write an elderly stranger on the other side of the Atlantic to ask about her grandmother's extracurricular love life in the 1930s. Four letters from Albert had sent me on a twisty journey involving a mysterious woman named "Joanny," who appeared and disappeared like a sprite between the late 1920s and the early 1930s.

The *Mauretania*

As an oddball child in the 1970s who liked to collect old classical LPs, I'd heard of Coates (1882—1953) who was celebrated for his interpretation of Russian composers—logical as he'd spent his early years in Russia.

Since so many of the documents Dorle saved were love letters, I wondered if she had had an affair with him, too, the fact he was married no obstacle.

In January of 2016, I took out all the letters from the musty manila envelope marked "Coates" in Dorle's handwriting from one of the boxes of her items now living in my Brooklyn closet.

The first one written from the *Mauretania* in August of 1929 begins, "Dearest, holiest, grandest, sweetest Joanny, sweetheart."

I blinked my eyes and looked again as if the name could have been a delusion. Not "Dorle" or any obvious play on that name. Could Joanny refer to some long forgotten personal history between Dorle and Albert? Or be a different entity, a poltergeist whose letters had slipped into the back of one of Dorle's filing cabinets.

"This is my first love letter to you, my whole life's love and glorious Joanny. I am so filled with you that I am bursting with it. I could shout and scream and just pass out with my feelings for you … I love you so it chokes me to think it. It sounds all around. It reverberates with all sound."

Unlike Dorle's other master lovers, Coates addresses what were once called "country matters,") also known as "fucking."

"I need you. I want you, just to see you and hold you. Not that! Yes, that also, why not, no hypocrisy. It's all too true, all open between us, all mind, all soul, all of everything you possess I want."

The *Mauritania* letters reveal, if obliquely, the obstacles to Albert's love. It is, as John Carter described falling in love with his wife when she was married to someone else, "difficult to arrange." Coates had married Else Holland, known as Madelon, early in the 1920s and remained married to her at the time of the letters to Joanny. Geography is also a problem.

"I have ravenous ideas," he writes, "improbable I suppose but still such a comfort to think that you could come to Berlin … if you made up your mind to it …Why oh why had we to be so many miles apart 3000 awful miles and more? Heaven protect us."

Albert refers to the writing of a piece of music inspired by Arthurian legend, "our [his and Joanny's] monument, the Lancelot Symphony," a dramatic metaphor for their affair.

"Guinevere and Lancelot didn't remain after Arthur strode into the convent—I can't picture that—I can't do that with you. I must bring it to a finale with my belovedest as my water music rounds and rounds my soul, enveloping me and helping me to a mystic and everlasting finish …"

Madelon would reveal herself as I continued to read the letters. She was sweet, self-effacing, not at all like Arthur bursting into a convent to catch his wife in the act.

At four p.m. the following day, August 22, 1929, Albert still bursts with epistolary passion.

"I cry to you all the time! You know where I had my photo taken on the top deck and then we went high onto the skylight deck. There I traipse up and down up and down every night after dinner. I call it my holy of holies because Joanny was with me there and I had her in my arms."

Only mysterious fragments remain of the third and final letter from that late twenties *Maure-tania* passage.

"That's what you called me as I am you and you me … Your guides would change places with one of mine and this brings us closer than life itself through communication of our spirit friend. … Think only of your love and you will know your beloved."

Was signing "myself through communication of our spirit friend" a metaphor for their intense spiritual connection? Was the "spirit friend" an actual person who played some role in their lives. Dorle herself, perhaps?

Berlin

In April of 1930, Albert telegrams Dorle (yes, Dorle, not Joanny) to beg for a visit, but nothing suggests he received one. He next writes Joanny (not Dorle) in late December of the same year from Berlin, where he had hoped (in the *Mauretania* letters) they would rendezvous.

In Germany, Coates litters his letter with German, and his tone sounds more distant.

"I love you so quite intensely more so than you think and my *schweigen* (silence) is only because I'm working hard and always wait until I have something concrete to tell you."

Could "concrete" mean commitment?

If so, this could be the birth of a whole new trope. Dorle might have radicalized an old cliché.

We're all familiar with the idea of the woman begging for commitment from the recalcitrant man, but not the idea of a woman begging for commitment from several men at the same time, all of whom she happens to be sleeping with, most of whom happens to be married to somebody else.

Dorle receives another letter from Berlin at about that time (January, 1930) from an old friend named Henry.

"Coates is back in Berlin and I've been sitting listening to your praises by the hour," Henry explains. "At ten-minute intervals he even dragged out a much-used letter from you and read it (don't worry) to himself."

Dorle skirted the globe, but her social world seemed remarkably small. It seems perfectly normal for John Franklin Carter to meet someone she knows on a cut-rate Bermuda booze cruise or for Coates to run into a close friend of hers in Berlin.

Henry's letter doesn't solve the mystery of Joanny but reveals that Coates had strong feelings for the actual Dorle.

"This letter," Henry goes on, "is simply to tell you … not to listen to anything Helen and I have to say on the subject … to do whatever the hell you please."

Helen, another old friend, has apparently judged Dorle's freewheeling sexuality, but Henry complains "she's got so Goddamn many bourgeois prejudices and nice puritanical ideas … and she's such a sentimental idiot … she even told me in a confidential moment that she and Oreste only look at the aesthetic side of sex … I wanted to say that maybe that explained her headaches, but I didn't."

Madelon

Albert next writes Joanny in September of 1931, again from the *Mauretania*, in a distinctly less ecstatic frame of mind, to complain about a terrible boil which had become "a real dragon with so many heads called 'carbuncles,'" and mentions his wife, Madelon, for the first time in these letters.

"I'm only worried how Madelon is taking it. It breaks into our plans so very much."

So Coates writes his "holiest, grandest, sweetest" love to express concern that his wife has been inconvenienced by his boil.

Each set of love letters presents the same problem, trying to put together a puzzle with half the pieces missing, the letters that Dorle wrote her lovers. But the Coates letters are even harder to fathom because there are so few of them, and so many were addressed to Joanny.

Handwriting

There was something strange about the next letter, unfamiliar, both in handwriting and tone.

"I feel a perfect wretch that I haven't answered your letter long ago and can only plead that there was so much to do as soon as the holidays were over and trust that you will forgive me."

"You wrote me such a sweet letter, and really I don't feel that I in the least deserve all the nice things you said in it! You made me very happy telling me that you much enjoyed your visit here and that you loved our lake. I am so glad that the rest did you good."

But I hadn't concluded that the clearer, neater, school-girlish writing could not be Albert's until the phrase "from all Albert has told me about you" compelled me to flip to the end of the letter and discover that it is from Madelon, that what Dorle received in 1932 might have been an affectionate letter from her lover's wife, who goes as far as to say that she has developed "a real friendship and affection for you."

Another clue that I could have picked up on in the beginning of the letter was that it was addressed to Dorle, not Joanny.

"My only regret was that we didn't have more time together because you see I wanted you to like me too. People very seldom like me at first, this is my fault because I am too reserved.

"Life as an artist's wife makes one so. One gets so used to putting oneself entirely in the background and always thinking of someone else first that one's own self gets buried deep down inside of one."

Has she placed herself so far in the background as to entertain her husband's mistress, or has she no idea, Dorle and Albert dancing circles around her?

Shrugging off her melancholic introspection, Madelon talks about the weather: a tremendous storm on Lago Maggiore that destroyed one of their boats.

At least for the moment, we've got our characters pinned down to a place and a time. Lago Maggiore, 1932. Joanny is notably absent, but Joanny might not be Dorle at all, some entirely different entity that we haven't yet met

"I really mustn't bother you anymore. This letter is an abuse when you are probably busy to the eyes."

"Lots of love,' she concludes, "think of us sometimes."

I felt terrible for Madelon, dedicated to her husband, kind to her guest, unaware of her troubled future, a war about to sweep through Europe, her husband about to leave her for another woman — a South African soprano already performing with him by the time of this letter with the dramatic stage name of Vera de Villiers.

And on the exact same day also, of course, from Lago Maggiore, Albert writes a letter on his personal stationary addressed to Dorle, who is still "darlingest" but somehow no longer Joanny, in which he complains about the "empty void" she left in her wake.

A week or so before on a sultry summer evening, Dorle's last with the Coateses, the three of them drink martinis on lounge chairs looking out over the lake.

Mist rises from the water, but no clouds dot the sky.

Their Italian cook has prepared the meal though they are not yet ready to eat.

Albert's topic tonight is Scriabin, the Russian composer, his *Poem of Ecstasy.*

"Demented," he propounds, "erotic."

Madelon nods faintly in approval despite the dangerously sexual direction of the conversation, and Dorle looks warmly from one Coates to the other. At first, the situation had unnerved her, time spent with her lover's wife. Helen's disapproval, bourgeois as it was, has gotten under her skin. But as the days have gone by—Madelon reserved but not unfriendly, Albert ebullient as if nothing were amiss—Dorle has grown more relaxed, the alcohol doing its bit.

When Madelon wants to know "what happened with your opera about Scriabin, dear?" Albert stiffens and petulantly clears his throat, but before he can bristle, Dorle breaks into the conversation to congratulate him on such an "original" subject.

And Madelon rescues herself by praising the overture, the only part she's seen of the abandoned score.

Regaining his equilibrium, Albert admits that he's allowed other projects to get in the way and smiles weakly at his wife to apologize for the volley that's been thankfully averted.

And Madelon looks towards Dorle and smiles herself, grateful that her husband's mistress has contained her husband's temper, grateful that this young woman who works with Toscanini has been sweet and mild-mannered, not the brassy, self-important American that she'd imagined.

Dorle draws a sharp breath. However sophisticated one may be, this has all been stressful. The following day she leaves to join Maestro in Milan, so she doesn't have much more to endure.

Just at that moment, the sweet-faced Neopolitan lad who serves as waiter arrives with a fresh pitcher of martinis, and the sharply sweet alcohol water settles all three of their temperaments.

Vera

We must leave Dorle there as Albert's letter from Lago Maggiore is the last of the Coates's missives chronologically, and my research into the conductor's life had dead ended.

"The Google," as an elderly Italian relative calls it, can be moody and unpredictable. Of course, I'd searched Coates and Dorle, Dorle and Coates in every imaginable iteration using Google and several other databases, but when I finally searched for Coates's second wife, Vera de Villiers, something interesting emerged. "VILLIERS, VERA DE (Johanna Véronique Waterston Graaff, Mrs Albert Coates), dramatic mezzo-soprano, born 26 September 1891 in Cape Town."

Could it really be just a coincidence that Albert wrote the letters in my possession to Joanny when his next wife would be named Johanna? Could all the passion from the *Mauretania* really be intended for her? Johanna (I'll call her Vera to avoid confusion) had performed with Coates as early as 1932, only two years after the first letters, and they certainly could have met before then. The time at Lago Maggiore might not have been so fraught if Dorle was not really Albert's mistress.

But if the letters were for Vera, how did they end up in Dorle's possession? Albert's odd reference to a "spirit friend" raises the possibility of some sort of intermediary, but I didn't like to think of Dorle as some sort of former-day pimp, hooking Albert up with his mistress.

South African Answers?

Albert spent his last years with Vera in her native South Africa, and I learned that the library of Stellenbosch University near Capetown houses a small Albert Coates archive.

I contacted Santie de Jongh, the woman who runs it, in hopes that somehow something there might help me answer my question about Joanny's identity.

De Jongh seemed genuinely excited to hear from someone with letters from Coates and sent me a series of links to information about him.

Diligently, I made my way through them, even paying Google Books thirty dollars to download a tome about Wagner conductors which obviously had little to say about Albert's love affairs.

De Jongh did shine a ray of hope on the

situation, though, by contacting a surviving member of Albert and Vera's family to see if they would talk to me.

Meanwhile, I went back to the Joanny letters in search of more clues, excited by the thought that they may have really been intended for Vera. But New York kept coming up, pretty clearly where this Joanny was living, and while Vera's movement in the late twenties and early thirties are hard to trace, she didn't make her New York debut until 1932 and was presumably in South Africa when she wasn't touring.

And there is the letter from Henry to consider, the one in which Coates brings Dorle (not Joanny) up at "ten minute intervals," and clings desperately to a "used letter she wrote to him," pretty clear evidence of some passionate attachment.

All of which seem to turn Joanny back into Dorle and leave the Joanny/Johanna similarity in the realm of coincidence.

When the Coates relative didn't get in touch with me, I asked Santie for permission to get in touch with her. Santie got back to me in the middle of the Brooklyn night, the South African morning, with the email address of one Judy Hugo. How Judy was related to Albert or Vera, Santie did not say.

I was excited to contact a member of the family I'd been so immersed in, but nervous as well because I had no way of knowing who she was and what she might feel about the nefarious goings-on in her family in the late twenties and early thirties.

I thought the best approach was to first request permission to ask.

"In New York where I live," I wrote Ms. Hugo, "I found about a dozen letters to my great-aunt Dorle Jarmel Soria from Albert Coates. The letters are from the late twenties and early thirties, and I am interested in learning more about Coates as I've found very little personal information. I wondered in what way you are related to Coates and if I can ask you questions about him?"

"I don't mind at all if you address me as Judy as that is my name," began Judy when she wrote me back, assuring me that she'd be happy to answer any question she could. She explained that she was Vera's granddaughter and had some memories of Albert, Vera's third husband, though he had died when she was eight.

This was no obscure relative: the granddaughter of the notorious (at least to me) Vera de Villiers, whose name came right out of Daphne du Maurier.

I decided to ask Judy (who was in her seventies) some polite general questions about her grandmother and Albert, then find a way to bring up the delicate topic of her grandmother's extramarital affair before she, Judy, was born.

I thought about grandmothers, our classic version of them: more doddering than adultering. That family story about Grandmother Faie screwing Cary Grant on the Golden Gate train from Los Angeles to Chicago while her husband was in the bar car should have dispelled my notions of classic grandmothers, at least of Joanna's and Faie's generation, though the train story was likely apocryphal for a slew of reasons.

In any case, I knew it was doubtful, nearly impossible, that Judy would have much notion of her grandmother's love life, nor any real sense of the mystery of the Joanny letters. Nevertheless, I was dying to ask.

In my next letter to Judy, I started with a general question about her grandmother and Albert Coates. It was exciting to be writing a relative of one of Dorle's master lovers. The only other such person that I had been in contact with, Najif, Georges Asfar's son, had been friendly but elusive.

Slowly, I wound my way towards my question. "My real question," I had the misfortune to put it, as if my interest in her grandmother and Coates as she knew them was just for show.

"My real question is sort of a puzzle. Some of the letters I described from Albert Coates to my great-aunt were addressed to 'Joanny.' I had assumed Joanny was an odd pet-name Coates had for my aunt, but when I learned about Johanna, your grandmother, I was flabbergasted. If they were love letters he wrote to your grandmother, why did my great aunt have them in her possession?

"How ever long ago, these are still very personal questions, and I hope they are not offensive. I did wonder if you knew anything about the circumstances of Coates leaving his first wife, Madelon, and ending up with your grandmother, whom I know he didn't marry until the forties. Was she, in fact, known as Joanny? Could that be some incredible coincidence?"

First Judy attached a family portrait from 1952 in South Africa with Vera, Albert, and all the children and grandchildren, including herself looking very fetching in a simple white dress.

"Albert's pet name to the family was 'Bokkie,' which means 'little buck' in Afrikaans. This was by no means any reflection on his stature and personality as he certainly was a larger-than-life character and we were all very fond of him. Albert and Vera were certainly soul mates.

"Just to give you some background. Vera, my grandmother, was born in 1891 and grew up in the Victorian/Edwardian era. She married my grandfather, Dr. P.M. Daneel, a surgeon who had spent 10 years at Heidelberg University, Germany, at the turn of the century. They were blessed with 3 children, one of whom was my father. After the success of winning a gold medal at the South African Eisteddfod, she left for Europe to further her studies. She married her second husband, F.J. Nettlefold, in 1925 and their marriage was blessed with 3 children. F.J. did much to encourage her in her career as a singer."

"With the onset of the Second World War," she goes on, "England and Europe must have been hell to live in, and with two artistic individuals, I suppose the decision was made to transfer to the United States. I think they did this just before war was declared. It was also the norm for children to be brought up by a gang of governesses.

After all, they were to be seen and not heard!! Albert and Vera returned to South Africa at the end of the war in 1945."

Skipping entirely whatever happened to both her grandfather and her grandmother's second husband, Judy's letter raised several questions. By the point Vera and Albert were in America, Dorle would already have been married to Dario. Did they see Vera and Albert during that period? Could Vera—and this weird thought actually flashed through my mind—while staying with Dorle and Dario have grown suddenly nostalgic, brought out her old love letters from Albert and left them behind in the apartment? Vera and Albert did not marry until 1945, and I had now learned they were together several years before, which made it seem more likely that they'd been having an affair while Albert was still with Madelon.

"I have no idea why Albert's first marriage was dissolved, but I thought his wife's name was Elsa Lizzie Holland."

Which is true though out of some misplaced familiarity with the long dead, I'd referred to Elsa Lizzie Holland by her nickname of Madelon.

"My grandmother's name was Johanna, which is why Albert called her Joanny."

I don't know how carefully Judy read my e-mail, but she seemed to assume that the letters that I had found in Dorle's apartment were really intended for her grandmother and to confirm (could she really remember from that long ago?) that Albert had referred to her as Joanny. These days, Johanna is not a particularly common name in South Africa, though I don't know about Vera's generation, and my query to an official South African governmental archive about name popularity around the turn of the last century went unanswered.

"In closing," closed Judy, "I would like to say that my grandmother was a great charmer and certainly had charisma, dressed beautifully and always looked like a million dollars."

Judy was defending her grandmother's memory by painting a glamorous portrait of her and implying that she deserved to be presented kindly and fairly in anything I might write about her.

"I hope that the above information gives you some insight, but I really have no idea how the 'love letters' ended up where they did!!"

Purgatory

Judy had signed off, not leaving me much clearer about the Joanny letters. I also hadn't learned anything more about Albert's marriage to his reserved first wife, whose poignant letter to Dorle clutched at my throat.

What did the Coates do after Dorle left them on Lago Maggiore that summer? Obviously, they were both there to weather the storm (literally), but what about after that?

Albert waltzed out of town to conduct at Glyndebourne, or Edinburgh or Salzburg, where he might or might not have had other liaisons.

Leaving Madelon alone with the servants at the lake.

I have no better idea of what Madelon looked like than I did Sheila Carter, no images at my disposal. And all that comes up on Google-image is Albert's large, grandiloquent face.

I can't stop myself from having opinions, by the way, about my great-aunt's lovers. Albert and John seem full of themselves, while Georges seems sweet and Bill sweeter still, though if I were Irish or Arab I might feel differently.

A *Rebecca*-era Joan Fontaine but with an endearing pug nose and deep grey eyes, my imaginary Madelon.

A few days after Albert's departure finds her gazing out the window of her sewing room at the lake in the distance and the Neapolitan kid cleaning the pool. A cool breeze sweeps through the trees, swirling the water.

She feels deliciously relaxed but sad, somehow, at the same time. Really, Madelon, she tells herself, there is nothing wrong. Even if Albert had been carrying on with the young American who had visited, she posed no imminent threat with that busy New York life, which she would hardly give up for Albert.

Madelon's eyes water, but she does not cry. Change is coming, she senses, as the wind picks up even more, a reminder of Tuesday's storm, but then dies down. She does not know what or when. It will bring sadness, of course, but life will go on.

My mind slips from Madelon to Dorle, not

at the gates of hell where only the cruelest, most Old Testament God would send her, but serving a brief stint in purgatory before getting slipped the golden key.

A purgatory inspired by foggy London in thirties movies: hansom cabs, men in overcoats drifting by. And sometimes someone familiar. Not Georges, nor John nor Albert but their wives, the injured parties: Sheila, of course; Charlotte, Haldane's wife, and Madelon in shadowy ghost-like form. Each time one approaches in the distance, Dorle feels a chill in her bones, a feeling of disquiet. The fog dissolves as they grow closer, nod politely to her, and move on. No, it wasn't right for her to have done as she did, but she took no husbands away. And their husbands had other dalliances, each and every one. Perhaps they had more passion for Dorle than the others, but, for that, she can't take responsibility.

Tamara

There were no more emails from Judy and no more letters to read. I did not know how we got from Albert and Madelon entertaining on Lago Maggiore to Albert and Vera taking refuge in New York. And no clear idea, still, about the identity of Joanny.

I tried one last avenue.

In one of his letters to Joanny/Dorle, Albert refers to "my little baby." If he or she happened to have been a child, not a lap dog or other small animal, he or she might still be alive though in their eighties by now.

Judy Hugo responded to my question about Albert's having children.

"… have just met someone recently from the U.K. that used to have musical evenings at his home when he lived there. He is a man of about 80 years of age. Much to our mutual surprise, Tamara Coates was one of those that attended. When I next see him, I'll ask more detail. She is married, and I know that she was Albert's only child. My friend said that he last had contact with her about 20 years ago. Small world that we live in!!"

I couldn't wait until Judy Hugo happened to run into this man. I was in far too deep for that. Desperate for answers, I went on Ancestry.com, where I learned that her full name was Tamara Sydonie Coates. Apparently, she played French horn, married a man named Kenneth Hunt, and had four children: Elizabeth, Sonya, Tanya, and Paul. The dates and details matched. This really was Albert and Madelon's daughter, her husband and her children.

Ancestry also divulged their geographical locations, but they didn't really make sense. Why would the children of a British mother and a perfectly British-sounding father (to judge by his name) turn out to be scattered around the rural American South?

There were even pictures of her children, smiling broadly, looking relaxed, untainted by the desperate love affairs of their not-too-distant ancestors.

I had even picked out one of them, Elizabeth Hunt from Texas, called her number, got a working-class Southern voice on an answering machine, and neglected to leave a message by the time I realized that Ancestry.com was tricking me, or at least I was misunderstanding how to use it. The addresses were just suggestions: Elizabeth, Sonya, Tanya, and Paul Hunts picked at random.

After that, I scoured as many databases as I could come up with in search of Tamara, Kenneth and their children. Nothing, nothing, and more nothing.

When I tried poking around Ancestry.com again, I realized that I had only limited access because I had not officially joined, but when I tried to acquire a month's membership in their "International Traveler" category because Tamara and her family were most likely not living in America, something went wrong every time. The screen would freeze just as I was about to acquire access as if Tamara had conspired with Ancestry to deprive me of my rightful information.

When I finally called them up and gave my credit card over the phone and gained full access, I learned just a little bit of new information. Tamara Sydonie Coates had married Kenneth Hunt in Marylebone, London, and she, Tamara, was apparently alive.

It had been getting late, a September evening in 2017, and I felt more and more frustrated by the mysteries of Joanny and, now, Tamara.

Disorganized about the mailing addresses of my friends, I often check whitepages.com to locate them and tend to be offered not just street addresses and zip codes, but also (for a small fee) birth certificates, past marriages and criminal records.

Which offends me, but that evening, a few drinks in me, Angela asleep, our big yellow mutt gazing quizzically in my direction, I got over my qualms.

A public-records-for-hire engine in the UK located a Tamara Hunt, 85, living in Marylebone, Her father, Albert Coates, mother, Elsa Lizzie Holland Coates, and husband, Kenneth Hunt.

Now, I had a telephone number. And an address. Exultant, I fell asleep around three in the morning but found myself wide awake, two hours later, ten in the British morning.

Not drinking coffee, brushing my teeth, or pausing to pee, I ran across the apartment to our landline, entered 011, the international access code, 35, the UK country code, when my senses returned to me. There was no reason to bother an 85-year-old stranger by phone. I should write a letter.

Dear Mrs. Hunt:

I apologize for the presumptuous writing out of the blue, but I have some questions that only you may be able to answer.

My great-aunt, Dorle Jarmel Soria, who resided [note my anxious formality] in New York, knew your father, Albert Coates. I found the enclosed letters in her possession when she died. [I had copied and enclosed the Joanny letters to let them speak for themselves.]

I'm terribly sorry if these letters are a shock, but I wondered if you had any notion of the identity of the Joanny to whom he wrote on the Mauretania.

Sincerely and apologetically,

David Winner

I checked over my letter several times, placed it in an envelope with more than enough stamps to make it to England, and charged to the nearest mailbox before diving back into bed.

In the days and weeks that followed, the letter was never far from my mind.

Our friendly Brooklyn mail woman watched me anxiously wait for her to dole out mail to the various apartments in our building. I wanted to explain what it was all about, but it was too long and abstruse a tale.

Three weeks later:

Dear David Winner:

I won't pretend that your letter was pleasant to receive, Mother and Father dead all these years. I was indeed put off by your presumption and disturbed that you found my address. My younger friends tell me that nothing is private these days, so it should not have been a surprise.

Receiving Father's letter to a woman who was not Mother made me rather ill, but as I do have something approximating an answer, I have decided to respond.

Of course, Father left Mother for the South African when I was in my teens, but I would not have known of these letters of yours if it were not for the visit I took to Stellenbosch in the early sixties when I learned Father was unwell.

We took a short walk in their garden. Exhausted, he sat down on a bench and began to regale me with words about Mother, how kind she had been, how sweet, beautiful in her day, but then his topic changed suddenly in the way of the old. He discussed a Jewish girl he'd met aboard ship to whom he'd lost his heart. It was only after their affair was over, I gathered, that he lost his heart yet again to the South African.

Your great aunt, Dorle Jarmel Soria, was, I presume, the Jewish girl. Why he called her what he called her I cannot say but the letters you copied for me were surely for her.

Please do not write again.

Tamara Hunt

No, not true, not a word of it. As I couldn't stand the absence of answers, I made up what I could. My master lovers imagination in overdrive, I'd been making up stories about Dorle's lovers, but now I was making them up about myself.

The truth just seems so slippery. I'd have to be a fanatic believer in coincidence to believe that Albert chose Joanny as a nickname for Dorle, but I'd have to ignore geography, chronology, and the words of Dorle's friend, Henry, to imagine the letters were for Vera.

CHAPTER TEN
NOVELETTE

Could Dorle have really stayed with the Coates's while having an affair with Albert? That would be, well, terrible.

Teen Dorle whitewashed her master lovers (the violence of Henry VIII hardly worried her), but I don't want to whitewash Dorle.

She was party to adultery quite assiduously in the 1930s, but I'm more troubled by something that happened much later in her life.

More what she didn't do than what she did, a failure of vision that had nothing to do with her blindness, a failure born of race, class, and pride.

The figure of Novelette Ewbanks, a Black woman from Jamaica, appears several times in these pages. She served Dorle drinks and dinner when the "Chinaman" came over. She cared for Dorle when Dorle could no longer care for herself.

Dorle and Faie, like most of their ilk in New York, had people working for them. I slept in the tiny maid's room of Faie's Upper East Side apartment, as there was no live-in servant, but a woman from Ireland (whom I will call Marie) came twice a week to clean.

Dorle also spoke of Irish servants in her past as it seems that wealthy New York Jews may have tended to hire working-class Irish immigrants as domestics. Though women from the Caribbean would likely care for them if they got old and made it to the latter decades of the twentieth century.

Marie was warm, kind, but frequently tipsy according to my grandmother, though that may have been stereotype imposing itself upon reality.

I was frazzled, unkempt, not particularly attractive, yet she kept saying that I was charming and handsome like Prince Charles.

In any case, despite Faie's grumbling, she seemed reasonably pleasant to Marie. And Dorle was pleasant to Nancy, the *Chilena* who cleaned for her, and the trio of Central Europeans who catered her dinner parties. Dorle and Faie paid reasonably well, I'm sure. They knew the names of those that they hired and asked basic polite questions about their lives.

Novelette must have been recommended by someone in Dorle's circle. The elderly person for whom Novelette had been caring must have died leaving Novelette free to move on to the next person. After the last old person died, Novelette planned to retire with her husband, Cliff, to a house they'd already purchased in southwestern Florida, which could be tricky, as we never know when people exit the world, and Novelette was no longer young herself.

When Novelette first arrived, Dorle slammed doors and demanded that she leave. But Novelette stayed. Soon Novelette would:

Light Dorle's cigarettes.

Serve Dorle her gin and tonics.

Take Dorle's clothes off in the evening and put on her nightgown.

And vice versa in the morning.

Take Dorle to the toilet.

Wash Dorle.

Cook Dorle simple dinners not involving goat curry, stew chicken, or any "uncouth" Jamaican cuisine.

Dorle ceased to yell, stomp, and pout but she never

Learned Novelette's name.

Addressed her except to ask for help.

Asked her anything about herself.

Dorle treated Novelette like some high-tech robot.

Can we tie Dorle's treatment of this Black woman to the fascist ideologies that surrounded her in her youth? Did Dorle think less of Novelette because she was Black? Dorle's failing vision, hearing, and memory were convenient excuses, but racism was clearly in the mix.

My mother grew attached to Novelette. But she never questioned Dorle's inhumane behavior.

I didn't either.

Never once in those years did I ever say, "Dorle, can you say good morning to Novelette?"

I just accepted it.

The last time I spoke to Novelette was when I called her to tell her that my mother had died. Novelette had been very kind. I could have apologized for how Dorle (and all of us) had treated her in the past, but I think that would have made things worse. I just have to live with our failure as a family to do right by her.

For a year or so after the election of Donald Trump, I would occasionally wear a Black Lives Matter tee shirt, but I kept getting embarrassed when I ran into actual Black people because the idea of some middle-aged white guy's tee shirt telling you that your life mattered seemed pretty appalling.

In any case, Novelette's particular Black life had not mattered enough to me. At least not enough to risk angering the protagonist of these pages.

CHAPTER ELEVEN
THE WARMONGER

If Dorle ever, as I imagine, associated her real life loves with her fictional ones, I'm sorry to say that lifelong Marxist, Spanish Civil War-combatant and 1970s-style swinger, J.B.S. Haldane might most resemble that "lovable Bluebeard," Henry VIII. "Living at a time when religion was a farce and politics a corrupt game ... Henry had but one illusion-love. Time and again, with unparalleled optimism, he sought happiness and peace in the arms of a woman." Both Haldane and Henry were big men with big appetites. And both were radicals of different sorts, Haldane under the thrall of Stalin, Henry VIII beheading wives and kicking the Catholics out of Britain.

But Haldane was best known as a geneticist. He melded Mendel's studies on inheritance with Darwin's theory of evolution. Along the way, he found a cure for tetanus and first suggested the idea of in vitro fertilization. He also fought for the Republicans in the Spanish Civil War, and wrote a children's book whose protagonist, Mr. Leakey, traveled the world on a magic carpet, taming dragons and fighting genies. A "large wooly rhinoceros of man" (one reporter's description) the bushy-bearded, scarily exuberant Haldane frightened Dorle's "gizzardless nephew" (my father as a young child) by sending him lurid zoology books.

Dorle's lovers ran the thirties political gamut, from John Carter's ostensible "Hitlerism" and work with FDR to Asfar's fear of Syria's looming independence to Barker's defense of mandate Palestine, to Haldane, a lifelong Marxist and Stalin fan. Samanth Subrmanian, his most recent biographer, joked that he was under such constant surveillance by M15 that they were functionally his first biographer.

Barker and Haldane fought in the First World War. I doubt they met on the battlefield, but I like to imagine they ran into each other later.

Let's cramp them side by side in a second-class car of a train from Dover to London. Haldane is on his way back from a conference in northern Europe from which he wrote Dorle. Barker returns from his tryst with her in Paris.

Bill can't abide the silence reigning for the first few stops of the two-hour journey. He's haunted by the memory of parting from Dorle in Paris, a separation so devastating that the Gare du Nord, where they said their goodbyes, has become a "station of hell."

Of course, it's raining.

Which gives Bill something to say to the large, friendly-seeming bearded fellow next to him.

"Bloody November in bloody England" is J.B.S.'s gruff response. He lightly mimics Barker's speech as he tends to do when talking to someone more lower class as he disdains his own plush accent, the unfortunate result of an aristocratic Scottish upbringing.

Barker feels ineffably annoyed, as if what's been slighted is more than just the weather. His stomach juices swirl inside him, and he clears his throat aggressively without coming up with anything combative to say.

Haldane shrugs his shoulders and smiles ironically.

When the train discharges passengers at Staplehurst about half an hour later, the image of a certain full-figured American Jewess arouses both our seatmates. Bill (more modest) has her open her hotel door in her nightgown as she had on his first night in Paris while ribald J.B.S. makes her ride naked above him, her breasts entwining his beard.

The Dinner

We know that Dorle met Bill Barker and John Carter aboard ship. We can assume that her avid Orientalism led her to Asfar, and music-world connections to Coates, but how she met Haldane is anybody's guess. His first letter to her comes from Chicago, where he has just arrived by train, having recently spent time with her in New York. In America to deliver papers about sickle cell anemia, eugenics, and other topics related to genetics, he stays at the "definitely unswell" Hotel Weston near Union Station. When he writes on January 15 of 1935, his wife, Charlotte, is back in England,

and neither of Dorle's other lovers happen to be anywhere near New York.

Haldane addresses her as "my love," announces that he has "thought [of her] frequently on the train both while sitting and lying," and signs it, "yours most violently, JBS Haldane."

We don't know who introduced them but can imagine what drew them together. Dorle's charm in those days ("a marvelous woman and grand" according to the mining engineer on the Triestino Line) seems unassailable, and she would most certainly have been impressed by J.B.S. Though not notably handsome, with a prominent nose and craggy features, his research had already made him a celebrity, and his commitment to the Spanish cause would have captivated a woman who "believed in doing something vital in the world."

She also had something of a thing for Brits: Coates, Barker, now Haldane.

Present at a dinner party in the Upper West Side apartment of Dorle's boss, Alfred Judson, are Judson, his wife, the young Vladimir Horowitz, who keeps to himself as usual, several other musicians and music world types, and Haldane.

Mrs. Judson had watched him repudiate eugenics at a Natural History Museum lecture and had approached him with an invitation.

As Haldane doesn't quite fit into this musically dominated affair, and Dorle is known for drawing people out, they have been seated together at the dinner table. By the time the soup bowls have been filled from the elaborate Chinese tureen, they are deep in conversation.

Dorle wants to know about the enormous chemical laboratory that existed at the beginning of life on earth. Haldane expounds upon the topic, getting so wrapped up in it that his face turns red, and he nearly knocks over his wine glass. Enthralled, Dorle grabs his arm with her strong hands.

By dessert, she has him explaining the roots of the Spanish war.

Coffee and brandy have already been served, the party starting to disband, so Dorle makes her way over to Horowitz, with whom she's barely spoken, to find J.B.S. blocking her path and expressing dismay that he's learned nothing about Toscanini.

He explains that he's in New York for a good bit more and wants them to dine together at her earliest possible convenience for him to learn about Maestro.

Which is how it happens that two days later they sit across from each other at a cozy table at Fontana di Trevi, an Italian restaurant on 59th Street, eating Bolognese, drinking Barolo, and talking Toscanini. Hardly limiting himself to the standard queries, J.B.S. demands to know how a "hot-blooded Italian" managed to keep his hands off as "lovely a lass" as Dorle.

Unlike John Carter, the heavily flirtatious

Haldane displays his wedding band on his finger, and, once he's got Toscanini out of the way, directly addresses the topic, about which he imagines Dorle has heard rumors: his marriage to Charlotte.

The Scandal

The circumstances of Haldane's marriage to Charlotte was a celebrated story at the time.

Charlotte, the woman he would marry, was the child of Jewish immigrants in England. She followed her parents to Rotterdam, but came back on her own to Britain, marrying a man named Jack Burghess in 1918 and bearing a son (of whom Haldane would later become fond) named Ronnie.

She first met Haldane when she interviewed him for the *Daily Express*. At the time of the interview, she had been working on a science fiction novel involving genetics, a very new topic at the time.

The circumstances of Charlotte's interview with J.B.S. were pretty bizarre. When she arrived, he was in a bedazzled state, having just injected himself with his own blood for experimental purposes. Under the influence, so to speak, he expressed some outrageous opinions to Charlotte but was astonished to find, as he later wrote, that "the resulting paragraph in *The Daily Express* not only kept to the facts, but, as had been stipulated, did not mention me by name. For this and other reasons, I fell in love with the reporter, and my love was reciprocated."

While J.B.S. (the bulky Scot) and Dorle (the small-framed Jew) may look like an odd couple, they share one important quality: falling quickly in love.

"Being in love was all very well, but there was the husband to consider," booms J. B. S. while magisterially signaling to the waiter that a second bottle of Barolo is required.

Unless the husband was willing to admit to cruel and unusual, which Burghess was not, there needed to be proof of adultery.

Thankfully, there were detectives who handled such matters, and one was employed.

Charlotte could not abide the dowdy hotel they had chosen, but the trouble with changing venue was that they might lose the detective's trail and risk not getting caught in the act.

"Fortunately, I spotted the man, average-looking chap in a cheap suit," J.B.S. explained, "decent enough, even carried our suitcases to the other hotel.

"Except I had to throw a monkey wrench into the whole affair because when it came down to it, I couldn't make myself admit to a crime that I hadn't committed." After all that work, J.B.S. denied the adultery, but nevertheless the judge granted the divorce.

Explaining how one got together with one's wife was unusual dinner coquetry, but once the tale was told, J.B.S. twinkled his eyes and asked Dorle if there happened to be a spot of brandy up at her nearby apartment.

"Yes," Dorle answers literally while considering the implications of an invitation to partake of it.

Georges is far away in Syria, John is nearer by in Washington, but neither is rushing to see her. Haldane doesn't provoke the sort of passion in her that they do, but he's pleasant, solid, warm.

Once inside her apartment, he downs a tumbler of good cognac, rises to his feet, and towers above her.

"Come on, dear girl," he commands like she's a small child or domestic animal, and Dorle allows herself to be buried in his large arms, braced by his firm embrace. His whiskers scratch, his mouth tastes of booze, but there's satisfaction to be had in his own satisfaction. Georges and John were such hesitant creatures in comparison, and Coates would get so emotional about the whole thing that she'd find him weeping afterwards.

When they are finished, and J.B.S. is dressing to return to the hotel, there is no awkward business about a wife in England because he's made no bones about it in the first place.

We know Dorle and J.B.S. spent a fair bit of time together in New York that winter because later he reminds her that he had "repeatedly climbed [her] stairs."

Okapis and Manatees

J.B.S. doesn't write Dorle for over six months after his visit to America, but the moment she shows up in Europe, he picks up his pen. He writes to her on the SS. *Lafayette* docked in Le Havre to cajole her into visiting him in England, even offering to postpone surgery to make himself available.

"Is there still any chance of your coming? If so, I can very easily arrange to be in London ... But please let me know fairly soon, as I do like to make some plans. For example, I am thinking of going to hospital for an operation about September 6th or so but could easily put it off if you are coming."

He drifts off onto other topics, climbing a "very small but steep" mountain and disliking Mozart's *The Abduction of Seraglio* on the radio, but goes right back to pushing for her to visit.

"Do make an effort to come if only for a week."

He cautions her about writing him at his house in Wiltshire: "I have so many letters that I get her [his wife] to open them, so don't say anything too private."

"But after all," J.B.S. concludes, "this whole letter is based on the extremely unlikely hypothesis that you will reply at all! Still you might like to see our okapi, manatees, megaliths etc. If so, you may answer."

The tone of letters can be deceptive. How gentle is his ribbing? How annoyed is he by her lack of response?

"Your no less devoted servant than ever," he signs himself forgivingly.

A Different Dorle

Out of nowhere, it seems, Dorle contacts him to suggest a rendezvous. On August 31st, he responds by telling her that she is a "naughty girl." "I must leave London today, but could have stayed had I known."

This last-minute bawdy suggestion spawns a whole new Dorle in my imagination: flirty, capricious.

So we must add Haldane's coy, coquettish Dorle to the list of Master Lover-enshrined identities: Carter's wild, sometimes nasty beast, Georges's Oriental Mistress, Bill's alluring Jewess, and Coate's marvelous mystical Joanny who may have been someone else altogether.

Dorle's response certainly gets J.B.S.'s attention.

"I am staying at
Kingstead
Fort Hill Bishop
Wiltshire.

Can you come down there for a night?

I could take you in the car, or if you took a train to Salisbury I could meet you there. We are about 12 miles from Stonehenge.

Could you not come down on Tuesday, stay the night, and let me take you in my 5 snail-power car to Southampton (quite near) or Plymouth (a bit farther) next day. Unfortunately, I don't know your port or time of sailing …

If you can't manage this, send me a letter or wire and I will come up to London.

"Yours in great haste," he signs himself, "Jack Haldane."

To rehash, he's called Dorle a "naughty girl," told her not to write anything personal that might alert his wife, and offered to go to what seem like extraordinary lengths to hook up with her.

But his postscript bewilders.

"My mustache is short and my head shines red like a lobster. The house is large and there will be at least two other people there besides Charlotte and myself."

Not the mustache and shiny head but the suggestion that (yet again) we find ourselves landing prematurely in seventies swinger territory. After all that flirtation, J.B.S. invites Dorle to a house party that includes his wife. But while we don't know much about the marriages of Dorle's other thirties lovers, Subramanian suggests that Haldane and Charlotte's "may have turned open by mutual consent." A few years later, J.B.S. will complain of only ever seeing Dorle once since 1934, their New York episode. I think it was 1935 in England that they met for a second and final time.

Plymouth

Dorle has arrived at the ferry station in Plymouth in advance of her departure for Cherbourg, as J.B.S. has wired her of his intention to speed out in "Scarface," what he calls his car, to catch a few hours with her before she departs.

Dorle had peered out the window at the dreary Plymouth buildings she'd passed in the cab on the way from the train station and ruled out the option of dashing out to some dreadful hotel for what had not yet come to be known as a quickie. Her feelings for him are more filial than sexual, the warm, humorous father she never got to have.

The Plymouth ferry station is equipped with one of those meager English eating establishments that no one who has ever been anywhere near France or Italy would call a "café."

She's drinking tea the way she likes it, in the English manner—milky, strong and sweet—chewing on a stale biscuit and trying to second guess Hercule Poirot as she reaches the conclusion of *Murder on the Orient Express* when she hears the loud sounds of a car past its prime, the opening and slamming of a door.

A moment later, a red-faced and windswept J.B.S. dashes in.

Relief upon finding Dorle sours into disgruntlement, the beginnings of distress, as he can't quite figure out what to say or do now that he's found her.

He peers through the open door at the rainy

outside, as if to encourage her to run away with him, but settles heavily into the chair across from her once she's gestured for him to do so.

Dorle breaks the tension by jumping to her feet, giving him a quick firm hug, and pecking him on both cheeks.

What she'd had in mind when she thought they might be in London together wasn't necessarily naughty but could have led in that direction: a relaxed meal, a bottle of wine, more or less the polar opposite of sitting at a dreary over-lit café while due to leave for France in less than two hours.

"A spin in the old Scarface, my dear," suggests J.B.S.

Laying a pound note, more than sufficient for what Dorle has consumed, down on the table, he grabs her hand and leads her outside into the mist towards his old and rusted green Aeroford two-seater.

Which naturally refuses to start, however furiously he cranks it.

After J.B.S. utters a deep, melancholic sigh and tries lackadaisically once more, the engine purrs contentedly, its fit of rebellion subsided.

"How much time?" asks J.B.S.

Her boat leaves at two, but Dorle says one. As he drives in Scarface through the wet Plymouth streets, no words emerge from the mouths of either of these loquacious characters. Dorle moves closer and closer to Haldane in the front seat, her small frame snuggling against his larger one, more or less the same satisfaction as can be

211

gained from sleeping with the man, minus the scratchy whiskers and violent ejaculations.

Limbo

After their New York experience, they had seen each other just once more, which might or might not have been where I placed it, 1935 in England.

After that, there were occasional hints of a plan to meet, but these are fleeting, unrealized.

We recognize this limbo. No longer meeting her lovers, just receiving letters from them.

Not so much with John, with whom she did not correspond for 25 years, but with Bill for several letters and several years, with Georges with fewer letters but many more years (their Paris rendezvous just my invention), with J.B.S. until he stopped writing altogether towards the end of the thirties.

The men in her bed become words on a page.

For years (sometimes many, sometimes few) after the affairs were over, the master lover letters continued arrive duller and shorter than the ones sent in the midst of their mating.

Except J.B.S.'s were pretty dramatic, as they involved the Spanish Civil War.

The Spanish War

What J.B.S. tells Dorle in his next letter contradicts Ronald Clark's claim in *The Life and Work of JBS Haldane* that "it would be unfair to say that Haldane enjoyed the little bit of front-line fighting that he saw or the experience of being bombed in Madrid … He was always quick to feel the suffering of others."

"You probably did not know of the bellicose side of my life," J.B.S. writes Dorle. "Indeed, it was 20 years since I had had a bullet fired at me. However, I found I had not lost my liking for it."

The reason he didn't feel "the suffering of others" was probably because he didn't believe that anyone was particularly suffering.

"The civilians in Madrid like it [the fighting] too, only one must not say so. Less than 10,000 have been killed or wounded in the air raids (that is to say less than 1%). The others are so pleased to be taking part in one of the greatest events in world history that they don't want to be evacuated. They have also developed feelings of fraternity and equality, which make religion superfluous. So a good time is had by all."

Haldane, according to Subramanian, his much more recent biographer, once declared himself "a man of violence by temperament and training" who claimed to be a descendant of Pedro the Cruel, the Spanish king.

The Death of Fathers/

The Strike of Elevator Workers

People died younger in those days, and if you took childbirth out of the equation, men died younger still. The death of fathers is a recurring theme among Dorle and her master lovers, starting with the "wild letter" that Dorle sent John Carter upon the death of her own, followed by the death of Georges's father, and on April 4th of 1936, JBS writes Dorle to let her know of the passing of his own.

"My father died last month of pneumonia, aged 75. I had a grand time trying to save his life by keeping him in an oxygen tent, which is all very well in a hospital but no joke to run in a private house. His lungs were decidedly better when his heart stopped, which was a pity, as he was enjoying life and doing good work."

While J.B.S. tried desperately to save his father's life when he was old, his father (also a scientist) had had precious little regard for his son a child. He tortured young Jack, as he was called then, like a latter-day Wile E. Coyote. John Haldane investigated the bends by lowering Jack down the side of a gunboat in a diving suit that barely fit. And experimented with killing rats with sulfur dioxide on another ship by sending Jack back down to the hold again and again to bring back the dead ones. John, who came up with the notion of sending canaries into mines, also had Jack recite as much of "Friends, Romans, Countrymen …" as he could in a coal pit filling with methane gas before passing out.

While clearly dedicated to his father despite those early experiences, J.B.S.'s words about his surviving parent, his mother, reveal precious little affection.

"My mother on the other hand has ceased to enjoy life or be much use, so she looks after herself carefully, and may live for a long time."

Haldane quickly dispatches with the subject of parents, dead or alive, and winds his way, via pneumonia, to the great New York elevator strike of 1934.

"If ever any of your friends get pneumonia, try to rush them under the care of Dr. Barach (I can't remember his hospital). Possibly of course, you and your entire family died of it during the strike. At least, however, you didn't have any dreadful climbs to do, as I have repeatedly climbed your stairs and know. I hope you got someone to stoke your furnace. But anyway, I was much cheered by the thought that you were not perished at the top of the Empire State Building. "

Not just elevator men but doormen, bellboys, pretty much everyone involved in the maintenance of tall buildings in New York had struck that March. Before it was settled by Mayor La Guardia at the end of the month, many of the recently built skyscrapers had ceased to function. Typical of that more radical Depression-addled period, the strike led to "violence and mass picketing" according to the *New York Times*. One of the odder events as when 32 tenants were arrested for staging a "snake dance," in protest, sort of a revolutionary conga line.

Haldane then proceeds to pepper Dorle with questions, including the perennial one about visiting him, and bemoans that "these apparently straightforward questions answer the definition of rhetorical questions because I don't expect any answers to them."

He concludes with a dry expression of love, "I may add that my sentiments towards you are unchanged though a little dusty in places for lack of any but imaginative exercise."

A Kind of Farewell

In his penultimate letter to Dorle, December 6, 1936, he wishes her an early "happy Christmas," announces his intention to return to Spain to help in the defense of Madrid, and makes a spirited apology for the movement, especially its importance for Americans.

"I don't suppose you have heard a great deal about this Spanish war, what with Mrs. Simpson and other important news. However, it is quite a real war and probably more important than most because there is a real sporting chance of stopping fascism at Madrid, and if we let them get away with it there, they will try nearer home next time.

"I indeed am inclined to think we may be defending American liberties too at Madrid. Anyway, quite a lot of people from your country are defending it. If you want to save my life, give a dollar for the International Brigade Hospital through the Communist Party. I don't suppose any other organization would be concerned on your side."

Now that he's got the possibility of not returning alive from Spain onto the table, he can bid her a kind of farewell.

"Whatever happens to me, I am sure you will remember me with affection. And I shall most emphatically remember the wonderful weeks in New York as long as I have any memories."

Haldane returns from Spain and remains among the living until 1964, the year of my own birth, by which time he has moved to India, but the finality of his 1936 farewell to Dorle may signify more than the realization that he might die in combat. He asks Dorle not to respond until she's heard from him, worried, I suppose, about a letter arriving from him post-mortem.

Yet, he does not write until several years after his safe return.

And when he finally does, it is only because Dorle has deigned to write him first.

"Things are looking quite lively here. We may have a war or a revolution or both in England in the next 5 years. Our government is systematically breaking international law, and thus creating a real revolutionary movement, which is quite a change.

"I should love to get over to N.Y. again. But how to do it is a question. I can lecture about anything: E.G. 'The Defense of Madrid' 'Royal Bleeders' 'The Nazi Race Theory' '"What's Wrong with Europe?' 'Is Materialism Dead' etc etc."

But nothing appears to get "done" by either party, as it is the final letter in Dorle's Haldane folder.

Which does, however, contain more recent documents—crumbling, yellowed obituaries of him from various papers. His death, I imagine, was greeted by Dorle with a sadness but also some satisfaction as her encounter with the warmongering Scot was probably, as she liked to quote her Horace, "a joy to remember."

CHAPTER TWELVE
"PLEASE DESTROY
MY LAST LETTER"

Dorle did not hide all the letters that she received from married men in her apartment. The ones from Arturo Toscanini were neatly filed in what had once been Dario's office. My mother discovered them after Dorle's death and donated them to the Library for the Performing Arts at Lincoln Center. I would have to go there myself to find out if there was anything to the family story about Dorle and Maestro being more than just colleagues.

I lost my bearings in the labyrinth of lesser Lincoln Center buildings until a security guard at Juilliard pointed me down Amsterdam Avenue towards the library. The short, somber librarian in his sixties peered skeptically at me.

"Can you be more specific?" he asked me after I'd told him I was looking for the Toscanini Archive.

"The letters to Dorle Jarmel," I blurted.

"She was my great-aunt," I continued, worried about giving him extraneous information.

The librarian did a double take and looked at me like no one had ever looked at me before, as if I were a celebrity, at least an unlikely ghost. A relative of the woman to whom Toscanini had been writing in the 1930s stood before him in the flesh.

"They're being processed," he said a bit

sheepishly. "They're on my desk."

"Can you wait?" he stumbled. "Half an hour?"

Five minutes later, he reappeared, bearing a large green folder divided into several smaller yellow ones. The first, from 1931, contained correspondence instructing Dorle about the details of performances, but in the second, from 1932, I found two more intimate telegrams sent to the *Île de France*, on which Dorle had been crossing the Atlantic and meeting John Franklin Carter.

"Thanks for the gardenias," read the more straightforward first telegram. "What a pity we are not together. Love from your friend, Toscanini."

"Thousand times," wrote the married conductor in the second telegram, "during the crossing happened the same to me, *tante carezze*." "*Tante carezze*" meant "many caresses," but I did not know what was the same.

The 1932 and 1933 folders also contained letters in the maestro's florid, nearly illegible handwriting.

One letter had the words, "DORLE, DORLE, DORLE," in large melodramatic capitals. "I cannot help myself to say," went a more intelligible sentence, "that I love my sweet Dorle."

Another note described seeing her after one of his concerts. "Yesterday, after my concert, I have seen your beautiful eyes well with tears. I was happy because it meant that you have been satisfied with the program, with the music, with my poor self."

"Dearest friend," the maestro concluded, "how I would like to kiss your sweet lips and embrace you with love."

I was putting the letters back in the green folder when I glimpsed a sentence in another letter from 1932.

"Please destroy my last letter."

Toscanini's biographer, Harvey Sachs, shared an anecdote with me about Dorle and Toscanini. "Farewell, thou art too dear for my possessing," she apparently told Toscanini. "Farewell, thou art too young for my possessing," Toscanini apparently replied. Our email exchange sent Sachs back into Toscanini's papers where he discovered a letter from Dorle to Toscanini that confirmed part of the story.

"If you should once again, feel the need to write me," she wrote, "I would be so really happy. You see when I left New York I thought of Shakespeare's words, 'farewell thou art too dear for my possession.' And so with my mind I gave you up. But not with my heart. And now I know that reason is not to be trusted, and instinct is a land in the dark.

Ever your devoted, Dorle"

CHAPTER THIRTEEN
DARIO!

By the end of the thirties, Dorle had mostly drift-
ed away from her master lovers. Had she grown
tired of tumult? Did she want time for herself? I
don't know, but we must put away for the moment those Master Lover versions of her: the
beast, the vamp, the Oriental mistress.

And return to a simpler more sentimental
one: the sweet, innocent story that is the only ac-
count I know of how she met and mated with
Dario, her last lover and only husband.

Dario left Italy and his job in the family
bank in the wake of the pact between Mussolini
and Hitler in 1939, which had frightened even the
most established of Italian Jewry, many of whom
left at about that time. Dario had worked for the
family bank in Rome, which was grand like the
one in Dorle's family. While "Jarmulowsky" remains emblazoned on a large building in downtown Manhattan, "Soria" was chiseled in stone in
another building right off the Piazza di Spagna
near the Spanish Steps.

Dario Soria arrived by himself in New York
bearing a letter of introduction to a New York
banker named Donald Stern. And Donald Stern
knew Dorle Jarmel. Apparently, Dorle met Dario
at a party thrown by Donald and his wife Maggie.

Soon thereafter, Dario was waiting tables at
the Buitoni (the pasta maker) Pavilion of the 1939

World's Fair, and Dorle was making her way all the way out to farther reaches of Queens to meet him at the end of his shifts. The two would sit outside on a bench and hold hands until the early hours of the morning.

After the fair, Dario got a job for the D'Arcy advertising agency, working the Coca-Cola Radio Hour show, starring the famous ventriloquist, Edgar Bergen (Candice's father), and his obnoxious dummy, Charlie McCarthy, while his romance with Dorle continued to blossom.

Which begs the question how her tremendous romantic imagination and appetite could be sated by one man. Marrying a species of refugee, however well-connected, may have fulfilled her desire to do something "vital in the world."

And unlike Carter, Haldane, and Coates, Dario had no wife. And unlike every single other lover, Dario lived in New York. Despite her European and Middle Eastern peregrinations, the city ran deep in Dorle's veins.

And only Coates (who may not have even been her lover) shared her passion for music the way Dario did.

Both Dario and Dorle spent their professional lives in the music business, and business as much as music bonded them together. Dario had earned the pre-War Italian equivalent of an MBA, and Dorle, while self-schooled, would wheel and deal her way to help create Leonard Bernstein and Maria Callas's American debuts.

Perhaps most significant is Dario, while stupid handsome and eleven years younger, was finally able to provide the commitment Dorle demanded so fruitlessly from several other lovers.

Mother should have been pleased as Dario was the only Jew of the lot.

And Dario was just so buoyant, even when I knew him years later, an old man with a failing heart.

My father worshipped Dario. "Elegant," my father's word for him meant not only clothes (wearing his Roman tailor-made shirts made me feel dashing decades later even though they were too large for me) but strength, courage, and love.

When there were too many Davids to tell apart in the Oberlin College of the mid-eighties, my friends started calling me by my middle name, Dario.

Which happened to have been a moment of physical and sexual awakening. I had spent the summer before in Rome, Dario's city, baking on the veranda of the apartment that my Grandfather Percy had purchased in the early 1950s, reaching some deep nut brown that could render me Italian, Arab, Latino and did not match my eastern European genes.

That fall—in the goofy, nerdy, hippie-like world of Oberlin—I felt exotic and attractive for the first time.

Starting that first summer after college and lasting for several more years, letters would arrive at my house addressed to some entity, unknown to my father, named Dario Winner: the first name of his recently dead and beloved uncle mysteriously attached to his own. Neither of my parents ever commented, nor did I.

Early youth can feel so mythic, ripe for romantic experiments. But in the late eighties after college, I moved to a grimy apartment in Brooklyn separated from my roommates by a lopsided Sheetrock wall. I struggled as an editorial assistant, a temp, a mover of office furniture, going back and forth to Midtown on the F and R trains, eating bagels with butter at diners. I was lonely, dissatisfied. Hardly any sort of Dario, I morphed back into David, who I have remained for many decades.

At the Stern's party and later, on the bench outside of Buitoni, Dorle and the real Dario's tremendous commonalities must have rolled off their tongues.

Italy, Toscanini, opera, family banks, an immoderate work ethic.

Composers such as Mascagni (*cavalleria rusticana*) and Giordano (*Andrea chénier*) kept their money at Dario's bank in Rome while mostly poor screwed Jews had the misfortune to bank at Dorle's.

Did she play harder to get with so charming a man without a wife who was clearly husband material?

No, I don't think she could resist.

And she did more than make love with him. Soon after they married, she nursed him back to health when he nearly died of pleurisy. A big scar on his back attested to the major surgery doctors had undertaken to remove the infection.

They lived together in New York, but he traveled often for work and wrote her letters from wherever he was. I soon located a manila envelope containing postcards, telegrams, and letters from the 1940s to the 1960s. Their correspondence generally concerned business topics (the Spoleto Festival that Dario was creating with Gian Carlo Menotti), but their loving valedictions could be outrageously saccharine.

1947: Next time we have to come here together otherwise I won't come at all. Because you are *la mia dorlina* and without Dorlina it is not worth it. love you *mogliettina mia bella* [my beautiful little wife] *Maritissimo* [an invented word that turns being a husband into a quality and means very, very husband or perhaps super husband]

1958: Dorlina Dear. Your cable arrived yesterday with the morning paper—it seemed to affect immediately my temperature which vanished cowardly when confronted by your affection.

Geneva: undated: P.S. You know it is very foolish after 16 years of marriage this urge we have to tell each other everything which happens every minute of our life. Hah! It looks like we are still very much *innamorati* [in love].

These words reflect my childhood image of Dorle and Dario's perfect marriage, a mutual adoration that seemed to exceed my parents' marriage and the marriage of my parents' colleagues at the University of Virginia as they faltered through the 1970s. And certainly my own relationships were proving more fraught and complex than those lovebirds on 55th Street.

But the illusion was shaken one wintry evening in the middle of the 1990s when I was having cocktails with Dorle and asked her a question about Dario. I don't remember what it was, but it took her back to the early 1970s, the period of my earliest memories of the two of them.

Calm and matter of fact, she told me that she wasn't sure of the answer; Dario had left her about that time for a girlfriend in Rome he had never gotten over. "Go," she had told him, "and return when you can."

I saw neither anger nor sadness in her face as she tugged on her cigarette, sipped her gin, and gazed wryly into the middle distance, but I couldn't wrap my head around what I'd just heard. Neither of my parents had mentioned it, and I had no memory of Dario being absent from 55th Street. I wondered if I should be angry with Uncle Dario, who hadn't turned out to be so perfect, but as I watched Dorle puff her cigarette and gaze dryly back into the past, I realized that I didn't have it in me. She had forgiven a father who brought mobs of angry Jews to her house and an unfaithful husband. Judging Dario seemed priggish and self-righteous, like some brash American character bumbling through the sophisticated European novel that was Dario and Dorle's life.

The manila envelope full of letters that I discovered from Dario only went up to the mid-sixties, several years before the affair, so once again, I opened the closet, removing the bike pump, the stepladder, the cat-carrying case and dug into the boxes brought back from Dorle's apartment.

I ran into familiar artifacts along the way: the many envelopes from John Carter in Washington, DC, Mandate Palestine Police postcards from Bill Barker, the postcards from Damascus and Aleppo brought back by Dorle in the thirties.

Sweaty and frustrated on a late summer day, I finally found another letter from Dario. It lacked a date and appeared to concern only business dealings until I stumbled across the following.

"I know that I love you. I know that only love could make you—of all people—accept compromise. Please try to think of all the good things we have. Think of them especially when I am not there. Whichever way the Chinese put it—the Yin and the Yen [sic]. With us the positive is infinitely stronger than the negative."

The clues had been subtle: nearly two weeks in Rome after a meeting with a conductor when Dario usually hurried from destination to destination on his business trips abroad.

When he returned to her, he was warm, kind, said all the customary things, but his grey eyes lacked their usual luster. He spent much time by himself in his study in the back of the adjoining apartment where Grand had lived until her death a few years before.

Dorle dug back into her distant past to try and place it. She thought of John, of Georges, the feeling she'd get when something was amiss.

Her suspicion could have ignited bitterness and cruelty, voices ringing ferociously around apartment 8D.

Instead, I imagine Dorle pulling herself together one morning at breakfast. Sitting, as always, across from Dario, she took a deep breath, a sip of bracing tea and interrupted his reading of the newspaper with a simple recitation of his name, "Dario?"

After decades together, habits long formed, even a slight irregularity would have struck him. They liked to concentrate on their morning papers. They seldom interrupted that pursuit.

The newspaper slowly moved down from Dario's face to the table, exposing his eyes, which would have looked apprehensively down at the ground for a moment before facing his wife.

Dorle's simple gesture, which would have been impenetrable to anyone but Dario, was weighted with meaning. She knew something was wrong. She even had had an inkling what.

Then Dario cleared his throat.

"Anna," he said. Or Maria, Renata, whatever she was called. A familiar name, a lover of decades past of whom he had spoken. Who lived in Rome.

No more explanation would have been required, and Dorle—who in the 1930s had terrified poor John Carter with her terrific temper and (two decades hence) would ban my mother from her apartment—rose to the occasion.

She considered her romantic education—the five master lovers of the 30s, Mowgli, Iturbi and all the other men she had known since she became "feminine," as she put it in her 1916 diary, and this sad moment in 1971—and decided to release him.

"Go," she told him, "and come back when you can."

She could not stand to lose him, but she would not force his hand.

He left for his lover in Rome, but fairly soon thereafter (I never visited New York as a child to find a missing Dario), he came back to Dorle.

Less than a decade later, after surviving a massive heart attack in Indonesia and a smaller one in New York, he would be lying dead in a Manhattan morgue, and my father would be accompanying Dorle as she identified him. Later my father would describe her heartfelt exclamation when seeing his body as a cry out of Greek tragedy, "Dario!"

CHAPTER FOURTEEN
ENDINGS

Now that Dorle was long dead and her apartment sold, it was time to consider the last acts of her other real-life loves.

By the time Dorle met Dario at end of the 1930s, Toscanini was no longer firing off florid notes. At his last concert in 1954, according to my father who was there, the aging conductor lost his place in the overture to *Tannhäuser* and put down his baton for the last time. Dorle (not a weepy woman by any stretch) sobbed the whole way back from Carnegie Hall. Three years later he was dead.

His daughters, Wally and Wanda, Vladimir Horowitz's long-suffering wife, appeared regularly at Dorle and Dario's New Year's parties in the 1970s. They emerge from the shadows of my memory—small ornately dressed women wearing lots of pearls.

All that's certain about Bill Barker since he stopped sending Dorle letters and got invalided out of the military was that he died in England in 1971. We don't know what killed him or how he lived his life, but we can say that he died absent the passions of his younger days: Dorle, the Orient, the opportunity to be a fairly good policeman.

Drawn by the promise of Nehru's socialism, Haldane spent his final years in what he called "the closest approximation to the Free World."

"Finally, I am going to India because I consider that recent acts of the British Government have been violations of international law." Not only disgusted by British politics, he'd grown tired of British clothing. "Sixty years in socks is enough," he declared, swearing to only wear sockless Indian attire.

The poem he wrote about the cancer that would kill him begins as follows:

"I wish I had the voice of Homer
To sing of rectal carcinoma,
This kills a lot more chaps, in fact,
Than were bumped off when Troy was sacked ..."

Georges's son, Najif, who runs an antiquities business in Beirut, explained to me that Asfar and Sarkis had moved from Damascus to Beirut in the early 1950s. When Georges's new store in the St. George Hotel was bombed in the Lebanese Civil War of the 1980s, he moved to Paris but eventually returned to Beirut where he lived until his death in 1995.

After reading Najif's e-mail, I caught myself idly eyeing my bookshelf, eventually landing on a guidebook to Lebanon from the mid-sixties, which I had found among Dorle's travel books and spent hours ardently leafing through, picturing the enchanted era before violence swept through Beirut. Not one to buy guidebooks without visiting the places described in them, Dorle must have gone there at about that time.

Georges invited Dorle to Paris in his letter consoling her for the loss of Dario, but maybe their last glimpse of each other should have been in the Orient where I imagined they had first met.

Both long married to other people, they amble slowly towards each other on a sun-drenched Beirut patio looking out over the Mediterranean. She looks older now, a tad plumper, but the light hasn't fled her eyes. A contented smile fills Georges's jowly face.

"Don't neglect me sweetheart, and do write me," Georges ended a letter from 1936, "because I love you so much."

Dorle's lovers tried to master their worlds. Georges ripped rooms from Damascus houses and sailed oceans to sell them. Barker commanded a large swathe of Palestine. Haldane fought in Spain for the Republican cause.

But as they could not control Dorle, they could not control their destinies: Asfar fleeing political tensions in the Middle East, Carter never getting near secretary of state, Barker forced to retire early in his forties.

And while Dorle soldiered on past her 100th birthday, the bodies of her men gave out on them decades earlier.

John Carter, like Dario, was felled by a heart attack at work.

John had been in the National Press Building office in Washington while Dario had been archiving old performances in the back offices of the Metropolitan Opera.

After Dario died, I flew with my mother and

father to New York. My mother and I stayed with my grandmother, leaving my father alone with his grieving aunt.

I saw Dorle for the first time after Dario's death at the funeral home where shiva was being sat, and later at the funeral, which took place at an enormous Jewish cemetery far out in Queens. Eighty at the time, she looked crushed and defeated. I could not imagine how she could pick up and move on, but pick up and move on she did, for another twenty-two years. By the time of the memorial concert for Dario about a year later, she was back to her unflappable self, comforting the famously emotional Leonard Bernstein, who was hysterically sobbing though he hadn't known Dario particularly well.

A Furtive Meal

Percy, my grandfather, knew John Carter. Probably, they met in the twenties when they were both reporters in Rome. Dorle did not correspond with John for over two decades, and it may have been Percy who got Dorle and John back in touch.. When John did finally wrote Dorle again, he declared that he'd learned from Percy, that she had been "holding up wonderfully."

Percy (who died when I was ten) was a forbidding, unsmiling, mustachioed bald man who visited my parents occasionally in Virginia and (appropriate for the son of a Flatbush toy salesman) bought me cool toys. They could not have been great visits in any case as my father couldn't stand the man who had abandoned him at birth and waltzed only occasionally in and out of his life.

Percy, by the way, was also tough on his second wife, Giselle, a refugee from Poland whom he'd met in Rome in the 1950s. When Percy, Giselle, and their son, Christopher, lived together in Washington, Percy was so tantrum-prone, moody, and insulting that Giselle sailed back home to Rome, leaving Percy, in his mid-sixties at the time, with sole responsibility for his son.

Caring, vital, and warm, Giselle took care of me that Roman summer between high school and college but was always referred to unkindly by Dorle as "that stupid woman."

We need to look at Percy through the eyes of Dorle, a woman who loved men, particularly powerful, difficult men like the dashing young reporter who had swept her sister off her feet so many years ago and remained in contact with her old lover, John Carter.

Let's say Dorle and Percy met for lunch.

The late fifties were the beginning of an era that would reach its zenith in the seventies and peter out in the nineties, the era of a very particular kind of Manhattan burger joint. Swankier than your average coffee shop, they tended towards black and white space-age décor and served huge, expensive burgers. Places like The Beefburger and The Bun N Burger spread like wildfire through Midtown.

Dorle doesn't meet Percy for dinner at one of her French and Italian restaurants, or for cocktails near work, but at The Beefburger on 58th and Sixth. Dario is lunching with a cellist, and Dorle won't exactly tell him about her own date nor conceal it. She lunches with many people, and Dario isn't so interested in keeping track.

Percy is in town for a series of business meetings. The one scheduled that morning had gone unexpectedly long.

So Dorle has to wait.

A windy, rainy day, she stuffs her huge umbrella in the umbrella stand and finds a table for two near the window. She asks for a cup of coffee, slowly sips it. After ten minutes have passed, she orders her burger: medium well with cole slaw, a pickle, and The Beefburger's homemade relish.

It has arrived, and Dorle has begun to consume it by the time a flustered, soaked Percy dashes in, his cheap umbrella having been taken by the wind. Before pecking Dorle on the cheek in his severe way, he takes a handkerchief from his pocket and mops the rain from his pate.

Then sits down without even shaking Dorle's hand or inquiring about Dario, Grand, or even Faie, the way one should, or asking the question he's been tasked to ask. Without preamble, he launches in.

A few years later, on another dark and stormy day, he will deliver an updated version of the same speech to my father and my pregnant mother. So dark, so cataclysmic as to drive my sensitive mother from the room, tears in her eyes.

But back to the The Beefburger in 1959.

Eisenhower may be duplicitous and jingoistic, Percy bitterly declares, but his absence will create a dangerous vacuum for whomever replaces him. The Russians and their Cuban puppets are on a warpath, a conflagration due to occur that will make Hiroshima and Nagasaki pale by comparison.

"Not just in that way but in all ways," a phrase Percy enjoys, "the world grows darker by the day." Decolonizing Africa, the Middle East, and perhaps the sub-continent are set to explode or implode. Latin America descends into communism or dictatorship. Europe rises from the mire of the war, but will collapse far worse than before, the United States too busy with its own degradation to come to the rescue.

When the old Irish waitress comes back for the third time, she boldly interrupts Percy to demand his order. They can't hold a table forever just because a man has to lecture about Armageddon.

Percy snarls, blinks, then looks puzzled around him as if he's forgotten where he is. He's been carrying on again. All women hate that, not just his wife, and he has to contain himself. People don't care how doomed the world is, how gangrenous, and the ignoring of niceties has cost him in the past.

After sullenly ordering a cup of coffee, he requests the requisite updates.

Dario: Fine but worried about Maria now

that Onassis is on to Jacqueline Kennedy. And poor Meneghini, her abandoned husband, calls every month or so from Italy as if Dorle and Dario could somehow patch things up between him and Callas.

Grand: Aging, a bit forgetful, but nearly recovered from her recent health scare.

Faie: Back in New York after the collapse of her California marriage.

Here Percy allows his eyes to roll as he and Dorle have agreed before about Faie's narcissism.

But annoyed by his late arrival and relentless monologue, Dorle refuses to indulge him.

Then Percy remembers what he's been dispatched to say, a communiqué of sorts. He'd run into John Carter, his old friend from Rome, on Capitol Hill, the man with whom Dorle "passed time" in the 1930s. John had wanted to know if correspondence from him would be welcome after all those years.

Dorle thinks of Dario and Dario's own flirtations. And thinks of John during their early years together.

And encourages Percy to encourage John Carter to drop her a line.

In any case, John picked up the thread again in 1959, discussing the publication of his latest book. He listed places where it had been "enthusiastically reviewed" but complained of the "stony silence" of other venues, boasting of his accomplishments and admitting his insecurities as if no time had passed between communications.

The last meeting between Dorle and John was bittersweet. I learned of it from a letter he sent her in 1960, written on Nixon-Lodge campaign stationary, as the accused Hitlerist and dutiful New Dealer had become a Republican.

"It was kind of you and your husband to give me such delicious martinis and so pleasant a reception," he began, formal and appropriate.

But his tone changed as he described taking leave of Dorle. "When the elevator arrived, and I was about to deliver myself of a profound remark —at least if not really profound, one which represents a good many years reflection. So for what it is worth it is that people never fall out of love. Sometimes love falls out of people, but only if the love or the people are not real." His last words to Dorle are not about Nixon or Roosevelt or Goering (or Black and Tans, Arabs, or Jews) but about love, which was, from early childhood, her true obsession.

If Goering, Roosevelt and Nixon were his temporary masters, Dorle was his constant mistress. He stayed with his wife but never stopped loving Dorle. Dorle, on the other hand, had long moved on.

When my mother, already struggling with Parkinson's, and I toasted Dorle's 100th birthday in December of 2000, Dorle asked how old she was.

"Fancy that," she said when we told her.

One afternoon in the fall of 2002, I returned

home to my Brooklyn apartment to see my answering machine flashing.

My father's matter-of-fact-sounding voice broke the taboo about bad news delivered by voice message. "Leave me in peace," Dorle had told me when I had attempted to hug her a few weeks before.

"Hi, this is Daddy. Dorle has died." He didn't have to tell me that I needed to make my way immediately to Midtown.

Upon arrival, I expected to be comforted by a tearful Novelette. But given how she'd been treated by Dorle, I shouldn't have been surprised not to find her upset by Dorle's death. She took me immediately into the room where Dorle had been laid out with her hands crossed over her chest like one of her fallen romantic heroes. After swallowing a teaspoon of broth, Novelette explained, she had vomited, collapsed on the floor, and expired.

It seemed ridiculous to call 911 as someone that old and obviously dead hardly constituted an emergency, so we left a message for her doctor instead.

While waiting for him to get back to us, I helped Novelette take care of Dorle's body in what I assumed to be the Jamaican way, closing her eyes and mouth. Her eyes were easy enough, but her mouth refused to cooperate as her lower lip had been jutting out slightly her entire life, something that Bill Barker had referred to 70 odd years before. Eventually, we tied it closed with one of her scarves.

We sat in her bedroom watching closely

over her as if she might reawaken and try to get out of bed.

Later, when I learned about her affairs, I wondered what it might have been like if she had died before her lovers. I saw Dario, John, Georges, Mowgli, pass tremulously by her body—not inside a coffin in an antiseptic funeral parlor, but on the bed in which they had made love to her. They were all long dead, but at least one man in her life, I noted with relief, had gotten there right after she slipped away.

Dorle's doctor finally called back and told us to call 911, after all. A moment later, as police and ambulance sirens filled the nighttime 55th Street, we thought better of our corpse tampering and released Dorle's mouth. It promptly opened again like a final surge of her irrepressible life force.

"The inevitable has happened," sixteen-year-old Dorle wrote in her diary after she'd lost interest in a boy. "I no longer feel the same."

I think of myself at that age, at later ages, as I am now, middle-aged, and wonder if I ever could have been worthy of her *Master Lovers*. Could I ever have infiltrated her dazzling, dangerous world.

Knowing so much about her and her lovers, I imagine myself playing with the past. I could prevent Bill Barker from catching the Triestino ferry, board myself, and take on some weathered war veteran persona. Or learn Arabic, approach her outside of the Philharmonic during one of her rare romantic respites, and promise to take her to Bagdad, Cairo, someplace she hadn't yet visited in her beloved Orient.

In any case, it was I in the end, not John, nor Georges, nor even Dario, who would take off her enormous bra, help her step into her old-fashioned negligee and tuck her in.

And watch protectively over her body as sirens pierced the night.

AFTERWORD

Dorle is over twenty years dead, her apartment long sold. The letters from her lovers lie scattered in boxes and drawers in my Brooklyn home, but I have no answer to a basic question about her. Deborah Baker's *The Convert* chronicles a Jewish woman who gets enmeshed in jihadism. The discovery of George Viereck's name late in the long process of writing these pages, the realizations of who he was and what he did, makes me wonder if Dorle's relationship with Viereck's friend John Carter gives her story some of the same reverberations. Should this bear a lurid title, *The Nazi Lover*?

A crucial part of the story is lost in the silence at the heart of this book, Dorle's words to her lovers. The letters that flew from her Midtown Manhattan apartment out into the world may also lie hidden in nooks and crannies somewhere, but nooks and crannies inaccessible to me. I can't rewind history to find out exactly what Dorle found in John Franklin Carter, but I can try to shine a light on him to try to grasp who he really was and what he really believed.

A Zelig figure, Carter's contradictory identity has morphed as I've learned more about him. Mild-mannered murder mystery writer and minor New Dealer ostensibly recruited by Goering to bring Hitlerism to American shores. Attender of Hitler rallies, friends with Hitler allies (Giereck, Hanfstaengl), but also FDR's personal spy against

German agents and a columnist who screamed in a *Washington Evening Star* editorial at the end of the 1930s that the FBI should focus on fascism rather than communism.

Bradley Hart, a historian who worked on Rachel Maddow's *Ultra* podcast about German infiltration of America in the lead-up to the Second World War, responded to my emailed cry for help by suggesting something basic. Answers might lie in his FBI file.

The only Carter discussed on The Vault, an on-line space in which the FBI has dumped declassified files, was Billy, Jimmy Carter's troubled younger brother, so I filled out a Freedom of Information Act request with the National Archives. After checking off the expedition box, as I felt myself to be in a hurry, I waited impatiently for a response, worried that they were too busy dealing with Trump's, Biden's, and Pence's classified documents to respond.

After only a week or so, an email arrived from the archives with files to download. Excitedly, I opened them up only to be rebuked as "the lack of expedited treatment could [not] reasonably be expected to pose an imminent threat to the life or physical safety of an individual," or "the loss of substantial due process of rights," or two other equally dire situations not relevant to my search for information about my great-aunt's long-dead lover.

With a weary and not very hopeful heart, I made another request without checking off the offending expedition box.

On my phone on the way back from teaching not long afterwards, just when I was least expecting it, more FOIA files arrived in my inbox. Another sharp rejection? No, John Franklin Carter's FBI files. A quick glance revealed only twenty-odd pages, but when I opened everything up on my computer, I discovered a novel's worth of prose.

He wasn't just combative with Dorle, I quickly learned, his penchant for conflicts had landed him in a lifetime of scrapes.

The more I read, the more his identity (Marxist, fascist, Republican) continued to transform.

My focus was his Nazi and fascist roots, but I found only one detail on that score. In the early 1930's, the Metropolitan Police in Washington, DC, concluded that he was an "organizer of the American Fascist Party."

But what was that? There was a Fascist Party, a group of pro-KKK southern Democrats who once gained some seats in Congress, and a tiny American Fascist Party, made up of Italian Mussolini enthusiasts, but John was neither a southern Democrat nor Italian.

When the Metropolitan Police's claim comes up later in the file, the phrase "which organization is not identified" suggests that the FBI could not place them either.

As that information neither vindicates nor exculpates him, I continued through the file, trying to get a handle on Carter.

After graduating from Yale in the early 1920s (where he chaired the Yale humor magazine, his first newspaper job), he spent much of the remainder of the 1920s in Rome: first as a representative of the Williamstown Institute of Politics, then, later, a correspondent for the *London Daily Chronicle* and the *New York Times*. Back in the United States in 1928, he got his first government job, as economic advisor for the Coolidge administration, and had his first brush with the FBI as "Articles revealing secrets of the State Department began to appear in newspapers and magazines under the name of Jay Franklin [John's pseudonym], resulting in an investigation."

Kicked out of the Coolidge State Department, he concentrated on journalism until rejoining the government in the early thirties after Roosevelt was elected. He worked with Rexford Guy Tugwell, the Undersecretary of Agriculture, from 1934 to 1938 on New Deal farm plans across the country.

In Carter's 1932 novel *Murder in the Embassy*, he created a fictional secret service working for "the liveliest cripple in American politics [who is] as easy to pin down as a live eel on a sheet of oilcloth." Apparently unaware or unoffended by that portrayal, eight years later, FDR granted Carter the authority to create what the FBI called "Carter's organization," in Bradley Hart's words, "a one-man intelligence service!"

Several times in his letters, he boasts to Dorle of having visited Roosevelt in his Hyde Park, New York, home. John's politics seem so questionable, his rhetoric so melodramatic, but he'd gained the president's trust.

Carter's organization initiated a motley group of projects focused on enemy subterfuge, though it's not clear that there was any "there there" in most of them. U-boats roamed the waters off Trinidad, but there was no particular evidence to suggest that the long-standing French community in Trinidad was really "vulnerable to espionage," and potentially useful for "counter espionage," as Carter believed. Nevertheless, he dispatched a French-speaking anthropologist named Henry Fields to fly down to the island. J. Edgar Hoover, Carter's foil as we will see, okayed this as long as the FBI was not involved, though he believed that Fields was "not very adept at evaluating the information he gets," nor a "good judge of character."

A larger angle of Carter's information empire involved investigating people in New York City with possible German ties, ironic given Carter's own connections just a few years earlier. There was Harry Stamford, who "dismissed anyone on the spot who made the [patriotic] V sign;" Paul Nerbert, "a fattish violist," who had been a member of the German Bund; and an unidentified group taking photos of British warships from the New York Bay Cemetery in Jersey City. Cherry Grove on Fire Island came under suspicion a few decades before its party days as a "meeting place for a vast amount of foreigners."

Another focus in NYC was the Café Society night club, an early integrated venue featuring African American musicians and the occasional left-leaning political gathering. An agent, hired by

Carter to investigate the club, racked up a $750.00 (1941 dollars!) bill. Carter tried to get the FBI to pay, but they refused because it was not their investigation. "Absolutely not," scrawled Hoover.

Carter also wanted to bring Putzi Hanfstaengl, the man with whom he and Sheila had traveled in Germany, from Canada to the United States for questioning. Putzi, trying to get back in Hitler's good graces after being outmaneuvered by Goebbels (and denounced by Trinity Mitford), had agreed to be parachuted down on the Nationalist side of the Spanish Civil War to assist Franco's forces. But after the plane had to make an emergency landing in Leipzig, Putzi realized that he was about to be dumped on the dangerous Loyalist side instead and escaped Germany. After being imprisoned by the British, he ended up interned in Ottawa.

Apparently, something went awry when John and Sheila Carter crossed over the Canadian border, because Carter asks the FBI and the State Department for assistance returning to America.

No one wants to help, a State Department official declaring that "in all probability, Carter, being the type that he is, insulted some immigration inspector on the way up and anticipates an argument with this immigration inspector on the way down."

Carter successfully brought Hanfstaengl over the border, where one of his contributions to intelligence about Germany were salacious suggestions about Hitler's sex life. Ostensibly infected by a Jewish prostitute with venereal disease in Vienna in 1909, he could never achieve "real and complete sexual fulfillment."

"While Carter was happy to associate with a racist anti-Semitic Nazi," according to Steven T. Usdin, author of *Bureau of Spies: The Secret Connections between Espionage and Journalism in Washington*, he was put off by Putzi's rumored queerness and put it to a test by introducing him to Gerald Haxton, Somerset Maugham's lover. "I wish you'd get rid of this man [Haxton]," Putzi reputedly declared, passing Carter's trial with flying colors, "one of the things I couldn't stand about Hitler was all the fairies he had around him."

In his role as spymaster, Carter had frequent run-ins with J. Edgar Hoover. Carter, under his usual pen name of Jay Franklin, published a satire of FBI overreach in the *New York Post*." In a spectacular raid early today, which wrecked the Supreme Court building, set fire to the library of Congress, killed seven and injured 32 bystanders, G Men, led by JE Hoover, director of FBI, arrested Associate Supreme Court Justice William (Baby Face) Van de Vanter on the charge of hunting ducks without a federal license ... Shortly after noon, Director Hoover without thought of personal danger, directed the attack from the top of the Washington Monument." Even while slamming the FBI in editorials, Carter pestered Hoover for assistance and funding like a veritable Bugs Bunny plaguing Elmer Fudd.

Hoover urged his agents to be courteous with Carter but to use "utmost discretion and circumspectness with this individual. Do not under any circumstances furnish him with official information." In a 1942 memo, Hoover wrote that "We know Carter well and most unfavorably. He is a crack pot, but a persistent busybody bitten with the Sherlock Holmes bug and plagued with a super exaggerated ego."

Famously, Hoover's suspicions (of Martin Luther King Jr., of John Lennon) were paranoid, insidious, but I think he had Carter nailed. That same self-importance and penchant for skullduggery appears again and again in his letters to Dorle.

There were fewer documents in the file after the war ended, the forties drew to a close, and Carter was no longer involved in espionage.

The focus began to change as well in the McCarthy era. Never particularly concerned with his fascist dealings, despite a story hiding in plain sight in the *New York Times* accusing him of running a Hitlerest party against Roosevelt, the bureau suddenly became concerned with his scant leftist ties, many from long before. Carter, it seems, had been a supporter of the Lincoln Brigades, the English-speaking communist army that was fighting Franco, at just about the same time that he was meeting George Viereck.

There were two testimonies against Carter in the early fifties. Mrs. Ralph Henry Graves of Garden City, Long Island, reported that decades earlier, 1921—1922, Carter had made "pro-Russian and anticapitalistic statements to me." Whereas Special Agent William Hershey reported that

Carter had appeared on the list of the Committee for Concerted Peace Efforts, which had been declared by the Committee for Un-American Activities to be a "communist front advocating collecting security prior to the signing of the Stalin Hitler pact."

In another example of the communist feeding frenzy of that era, the FBI also concluded that speeches Carter had written for FDR and Truman "plugged a soft policy against Russia." "The salary of a Marxian apologist," it is noted, "will be paid for by the New York State Republican Committee."

Marxian apologist, no, but he had become a Republican towards the end of his life.

The file was bursting with information, but Carter still seemed so slippery. I didn't like him, but I wanted to think the best of him, a figure of his times rather than some malign entity. I wanted to believe that Dorle was not such a bad judge of character.

Whatever the history of John's confusing relationship with Nazi Germany, neither the Trinidad investigation nor the expensive snooping on Café Society reaped significant results. Nothing near as glaring as his old friend George Viereck's attack on American democracy several years earlier.

According to Usdin, Carter sent Roosevelt "a never-ending flow of memos...consisting largely of voluminous, useless or absurd intelligence reports, harebrained schemes and gossip."

But Carter was also tasked with two significant inquiries. On December 30, 1942, Carter sent Roosevelt a 130-page report, compiled by the Polish underground, containing the first reports of the Belzec concentration camp in southern Poland, and news of "mobile extermination trucks in which poison gas was used to murder Jews." The graphic photos in the document's index forced even State Department anti-Semites to believe the intelligence.

Carter's most significant contribution involved Japanese Americans. It was he (on FDR's behest) who hired a man named Curtis B. Munson to travel to California to investigate them, as the possibility of conflict with Japan grew more likely. Despite a plethora of racist assumptions and terminology ("the Japs"), Munson was able to suss out the basic loyalty of the Japanese American (*"nisei"*) community even as his conclusions were tragically ignored.

Carter's involvement with the Munson Report appeared to place him for once on the ethical side of history. But I couldn't just leave it at that. I had to keep digging in my own inept way. Armed with Munson's name along with Carter's, I made another discovery.

The *Densho Encyclopedia*, an on-line history of Japanese Americans during World War II, claims that "a misleading summary of the report sent by Carter to President Franklin Roosevelt may have contributed to the report and its conclusions being largely ignored by the administration."

More specifically, Carter wrote that "There will be the odd case of fanatical sabotage by some Japanese 'crackpot'... There are still Japanese in the United States who will tie dynamite around their waist and make a human bomb, but today they are few...Your reporter is horrified to note that dams, bridges, harbors, power stations, etc. are wholly unguarded everywhere." Carter left out a crucial sentence in the Munson Report explaining that the "dynamite" statement referred to paid Japanese agents, not Japanese Americans.

Greg Robinson, a historian at the University of Quebec and a source used by Densho, confirms in his 2001 book, *By Order of the President: FDR and the Internment of Japanese Americans,* that "Carter minimized and distorted Munson's endorsement of community loyalty," as well as failing to communicate Munson's crucial distinction between the *nisei* and *isei,* Japanese born in Japan.

Would that disgraceful chapter of American history never have happened if John Franklin Carter had summarized Munson more accurately? FDR may not have paid much attention to the Munson Report even if he had read the whole thing. According to Robinson, he "seems not to be listening to information that was, as he admitted, 'nothing new.' ... He was in crisis mode, attentive to only immediate dangers."

Carter *was* concerned for the Japanese community, though. In the wake of Pearl Harbor, there was a wave of violence towards Japanese Americans, an antecedent to what's happened to Asians and Asian Americans during the Trump/

Covid era. Carter, Robinson's telling, urged FDR to speak publicly about Japanese loyalty. Along with Munson and Kenneth Ringle, a naval intelligence officer, Carter devised "an immediate plan of action in order to short circuit anti-Japanese violence." The Munson/Ringle plan involved asking pro-American *nisei* to "control Japanese property and organizations," so xenophobic outsiders would be less able to wreak damage. The plan, in Robinson's view, would have been extremely disruptive to the Japanese community, but less so than their ultimate internment.

While Roosevelt took only fleeting interest in the plan, Eleanor Roosevelt was profoundly affected by what was happening to Japanese Americans, announcing that, "no law-abiding aliens of any nationality would be discriminated against by the government." Gaining Eleanor's trust in this matter might have made a good excuse for John to get back in touch with Dorle, as Eleanor, whom she'd met several times, was a great heroine of hers.

In the 1990s, drinks with Dorle meant gin and tonics and Benson & Hedges. Conversation sags, and I ask her about famous people from the past, the two First Ladies she'd met, Jacqueline and Eleanor. Maria Callas, Aristotle Onassis, and even Jacqueline herself, all born after Dorle, were dead, but Dorle's face still clouds over at the mention of Jacqueline, as she'd stolen Aristotle from Maria.

And shines when asked about Eleanor.

Despite Eleanor's intentions, the Munson/Ringle plan was not enacted, in part (Robinson's view) because it did not come from official channels like the FBI or the State Department but from Carter's disconnected organization.

The decision to intern Japanese Americans comes up in Carter's 1947 novel, *The Catoctin Conversation*. Carter, Churchill, Hanfstaengl, Bernard Baruch, and several other men have a fictional conversation in a hunting lodge in western Maryland's Catoctin Mountain Park, a version of Camp David, one evening in 1943.

"In 1941," Carter has himself ask Roosevelt, "a government survey was made which showed that the Japanese Americans were fully as loyal as the Southerners or the Mid-Westerns."

"Why sir, I asked the President ... did you let the army [imprison them]."

Roosevelt calls it a "small matter compared to the war itself." And it is Bernard Baruch, the Jewish financier, into which Carter places more fiery words: "No arbitrary invasion of personal rights can be considered a small matter. ... Mr. President, you allowed the Army for its own reason, to commit a wholesale violation against the rights of our citizens of Japanese origin."

So when Dorle told her mother that she'd wanted to marry John out of a "need to do something vital in the world before it is too late. ... I thought through him and his political knowledge and connections that I could be of some small use," she was speaking of a man who appeared to have been (at least once) on the just side of history.

If we were on some mythic jury (or God or Saint Peter perhaps), would we find John Franklin Carter guilty or not guilty, heaven-bound or hell? He lands in a tricky place between fascism and anti-fascism, justice and injustice. A significant figure, particularly if you consider the lives of Japanese Americans, he was important enough to land on the radars of historians, but not so important as to attract the more in-depth analysis that could lead to a more categorical conclusion. For me, it comes down to that mythic trip to Germany when he was in early middle age, an attraction to Nazism that may or may not have fled him by the time he was dispatching spies to Trinidad and Café Society in the early forties.

And I continue to struggle to imagine what Dorle could have seen in someone so erratic and contentious. Especially when compared to the measured and elegant Dario.

Who shot cheetahs and enforced empire in his youth as an officer in the colonial Italian army in Eritrea. Hard to cast stones amidst white western men, particularly in the era of colonialism.

Finding a photograph of Carter from about when he met Dorle on the *Île de France*, I gaze into his face, his eyes, as if answers may lie there that I could not find in his FBI files.

He looks dazed, bemused, and his features seem surprisingly Semitic for someone of Anglo-Saxon origin.

Placing myself back in Dorle's shoes, I converse with John Carter while smoking cigarettes at the bar on the *Île de France* and take up his invitation to climb to the funnels atop the ship.

And land in a turbulent affair lasting nearly five years with that troubled and troubling character whose romantic rhetoric could almost equal Dorle's.

"That was a man," teen Dorle wrote about Paul Gauguin, "all absinthe and women and paint: the first his inspiration, the last his God."

"Sleep well, darling," adult John wrote Dorle, "your bones will remember me long after your brain is dust, and our words are a whisper in the wind."

Fascist, Republican, Nazi perhaps, but unlike her master lovers, he beheaded no wives, nor (Gauguin!) slept with any children.

"The longer I love you, the more I love you," he wrote her, "like a child growing big within me."

"On the walls of his hut was his last unfinished painting," Dorle concludes Gauguin's life story, "a nude of a native girl with flowers in her hair, a primitive Eve in a tropical Eden."

Where Dorle could have lived out her days with John if there had been no Roosevelts nor Toscaninis, Sheilas nor Darios.

About the Author

David Winner is the author of three novels, *Enemy Combatant, Tyler's Last,* and *The Cannibal of Guadalajara*, which won the 2009 Gival Press Novel Award and nominated for the National Book Award. His work has appeared in the *Village Voice, Fiction, The Iowa Review, The Millions. The Kenyon Review* and other publications in the US and the UK. He is the fiction editor of *The American*, a monthly magazine based in Rome, a senior editor at *Stat@Rec* magazine and a regular contributor to *The Brooklyn Rail*. Most recently, he is the co-editor of *Writing the Virus: Work from Stat@Rec Magazine*.

.

www.ingramcontent.com/pod-product-compliance
Lightning Source LLC
Chambersburg PA
CBHW022005080426
42733CB00007B/482